ON THUNDERING WINGS

D1279481

PRAISE FOR *ON THUNDERING WINGS*

"*On Thundering Wings* is a sensitive, challenging journey of faith that seeks justice and love for everyone. It addresses in a most personal way one of the disturbing issues in our church. I am grateful for the open, honest integrity revealed in this journey of faith. The willingness to open one's self to others in such a forceful way is a gift to be cherished and a challenge to be followed."

Jesse R. DeWitt, Bishop of the United Methodist Church, Retired

"This book is a fearless and open testimony based on personal encounters with the issue of homosexuality. It provides an uncommon inside look at how persistent cultural attitudes affect families and how church leaders deal with matters involving homosexuality. Roller writes from the perspective of retired pastor and former district superintendent whose life has been painfully impacted by this issue."

R. Sheldon Duecker, Bishop of the United Methodist Church, Retired

"Writing with passion and compassion, Ermalou Roller weaves the story of her life with the story of a critical decision for church and U.S. culture. She is at once witty and wise, hopeful and despairing, insightful and faithful. Clergywomen as well as all women who 'came of age' in the '70s will find part of their story here. And anyone willing to join the journey toward full inclusion of gay and lesbian people will have a companion along the way."

Sharon Zimmerman Rader, Bishop of the United Methodist Church, Retired

"This is a profoundly candid, insightful and moving account of a remarkable woman's emergence as a prophetic pastor and whole person, forced to confront and transcend the oppressive realities of abusive behavior both in the church and the most sacred of human relationships. The author's weaving of the story of her liberating journey with that of the church's oppressive treatment of homosexuals makes it difficult to set this book aside. Extremely well-written, it correlates the real and ideal in haunting ways—whether in sexuality, marriage or a church in divisive conflict regarding the heart of faithfulness."

C. Joseph Sprague, Bishop of the United Methodist Church, Retired

"Ermalou Roller's book is a powerful recounting of events in her church and in her life, which reflect the larger struggles going on in our society over questions like: What is morality? Is it unchanging, or do 'new occasions teach new duties, time makes ancient good uncouth?' Can a great denomination be open enough to the teaching of the Holy Spirit to change its positions on emotionally volatile subjects such as human sexuality? A truly engrossing story."

Jack M. Tuell, Bishop of the United Methodist Church, Retired

"*On Thundering Wings* pulses with the inner life of the author as she grows into an abiding commitment to the God-given dignity of her gay son, her courageous friends and colleagues in their advocacy for equal rights, and the places within churches that stand for justice in terms of sexual orientation. All around this tender and passionate journey lies the author's own wonderful and messy personal journey in which her own hesitations, inspirations, failures and insights let the reader know the richness of being alive. Ermalou Roller has let her guard down in order to raise the bar for discourse around sexualities and life in the spirit."

Hal Taussig, Visiting Professor of New Testament, Union Theological Seminary, New York; Professor of Early Christianity, Reconstructional Rabbinical College, Wyncote, PA; Co-Pastor, Chestnut Hill United Methodist Church, Philadelphia

"*On Thundering Wings* is a compelling story of a woman's struggle to find passion and truth in her life. This book covered many themes—among them feminism, theology, history, faith, personal integrity and society's changing and confusing expectations of all of us—and I had a hard time putting it down. I emerged with a better understanding of my church, my faith, my community and my own search for truth."

Susan Keaton, journalist

"For me to read something about anyone's life and about a topic like homosexuality over a holiday weekend, and Thanksgiving dinner and football games, it had to be GOOD. I had tears in my eyes in several places. Some of joy and some of sorrow."

W. Cliff McDuffie, Mayor, Zephyrills, Florida

"*On Thundering Wings* is a stunning narrative, examining the complex relationship between the church and the individuals it serves. Written with honesty and insight, it draws on both the author's role as a church leader and her profound personal experiences. Part memoir and part historical record, it's likely to challenge readers' views about homosexuality, forgiveness and acceptance of love in all its forms. The world needs this book and Roller's wise, compassionate perspective."

Debra Landwehr Engle, author, Grace from the Garden: Changing the World One Garden at a Time

"The personal work needed to achieve social justice, the pain and unexpected joy that come with individual growth and the myriad possibilities available if one pursues hope with truth and love—these are the messages that underlie this riveting read and make *On Thundering Wings* an exceptional reading experience for anyone concerned with these challenges."

Amity Pierce Buxton, Founder of the Straight Spouse Network

ON THUNDERING WINGS
Homosexuality, Love, and the Church on Trial

Ermalou McDuffie Roller

GoldenTree Communications • Winterset, Iowa

First GoldenTree Communications Edition May 2010
© 2010 by Ermalou McDuffie Roller

Published by GoldenTree Communications
1373 Hwy 169
Winterset, IA 50273
www. goldentreeco.com

Cover Design: Design Matters
Book Design: Gretchen Jensen

Printed in the United States of America

15 14 13 12 11 10   1 2 3 4 5 6

ISBN: 978-0-9785883-4-2

This book is dedicated to my beloved children:
Stan Roller, Kathleen Harkin and Michael Roller,
who have triumphed over their parents' mistakes.

To my grandchildren:
Michael Drapak, Jacqueline Roller, Julia Roller, Shannon Harkin
and McKenna Harkin,
who bless my life and the world.

And to my beloved late husband,
The Rev. Dr. Charles H. Ellzey,
whom I think of with gratitude each time I read these words:

one man loved the pilgrim soul in you,
And loved the sorrows of your changing face....

From "When You Are Old" by William Butler Yeats

TABLE OF CONTENTS

AUTHOR'S NOTE

In writing this book, I have quoted extensively from the official transcripts of *The United Methodist Church Re: The Matter of the Reverend Gregory R. Dell*, especially from Volumes II and III. I secured written permission from Bishop Jack M. Tuell and Rev. Gregory R. Dell, as required by church law, to examine and use these transcripts.

Other sources of information include interviews with Dell, Rev. Deborah L. Fisher, Rev. Fred H. Conger, Phil and Delta Stanton, Jerry and Ruth Moyar, as well as others who are mentioned in the book; the personal files and notes of Jerry and Ruth Moyar, Conger, Leroy Pickett and Rev. Duane B. Mevis; church publications; and other sources mentioned in the bibliography.

I thank my three children: Stan Roller, Kathleen Harkin and Michael Roller; my living siblings: Clarice Ralston, W.C. (Cliff) McDuffie and John B. McDuffie; the Rev. Dr. Tex Sample, Rev. Norma Lee Barnhart, Amity Pierce Buxton, Rev. Sandy Roberts, Carol Lysne, Catherine (Cathy) Mikes, Rev. Margaret (Peg) Schultz, Rev. Penny Thomas, Carol Wallace, Connie Miller, Chris Sheaffer, Susan Keaton, Rev. Bonnie Campbell, the Rev. Dr. Hal Taussig; Bishops Jesse R. DeWitt, R. Sheldon Duecker, Sharon Z. Rader, C. Joseph Sprague and Jack M. Tuell; and other friends who have read a draft of the book in various stages of its evolution and have offered invaluable comments, corrections and encouragement. I am deeply grateful for all their contributions and confess that any remaining mistakes are entirely my own.

I am also deeply grateful to Debra Landwehr Engle, who coached me throughout my writing process. She combined total honesty with considerable professional skill and experience as she offered her critiques. Just as important, she enveloped me with kindness and provided the encouragement I needed to keep going. I consider her a valued partner in the writing of the book and the best kind of friend.

I'm grateful, as well, to the excellent work of my copyeditor, Angela Renkoski, who improved the book in many ways, including suggesting the book's final name. And to Gretchen Jensen, for her page design and exceptional expertise in editing and proofing.

Some scenes (such as the meeting at the Chicago Temple in Chapter Three) contain quotes. These might not be the actual words that were used, but they reflect the truth of what was said according to the best memory of the person being interviewed or, when about personal experiences, my own best memory.

Scenes involving church security are partly true and partly imagined. Much was shared by those involved. Research provided more information. However, since the DuPage County Bomb Squad was unwilling to share their security procedures, the details of those scenes are informed imagination.

I have changed the names of some persons to protect their privacy.

FOREWORD

Rev. Dr. Tex Sample
Robert B. and Kathleen Rogers Professor Emeritus of
Church and Society, St. Paul School of Theology

I was struck when I started reading history that I could not find any of my people in it. Well, that's not quite true. They were the masses, the peasants, the working people and the soldiers, I suppose. But they were not kings and queens, nations and empires. They were also not the noted figures in "important events." It seemed like we were just around, kind of like wallpaper in the large room where important people engaged in historic happenings. My people then were often called "ordinary," but I knew my people were not ordinary; they were as extraordinary as anyone I had ever heard of. In a conversation on the street, in church, at the cabstand or at the fire station, they held center stage. So I wondered about history.

I felt the same thing as I read Ermalou Roller's manuscript. To be sure there are bishops, pastors, professors and laity here, but I kept thinking about the gay and lesbian "ordinary" people, who have struggled more recently over the past half-century to find a place in this society, in this history. Overwhelmingly, they are unknown except for those few (really) who get a great deal of attention in the media. Who will tell their story? Who will give voice to their "history"? This book is one answer to that concern.

Roller is not lesbian, but her life seems to occur in a vortex of gay and lesbian people. The tragedies of her own life, and they are not few, seem populated with gay and lesbian folk, and one begins to see in a different way their history. At every major turn of her life, we find a gay or lesbian person and a story of hurt and meanness, but also one of compassion and redemption.

This book is actually two stories, two histories, interwoven into one fabric. One of these, to be sure, got plenty of public attention: The charges, trial and penalty imposed upon the Rev. Greg Dell for performing a union between two gay men received sizeable media coverage. Dell was found guilty of violating the *Discipline of the United Methodist Church* and was suspended from his pastoral duties for an entire year. As told in this book, this story is a down-on-the-ground report of that trial, using the trial's transcript but also narrating behind-the-scenes events that occurred.

It is a difficult story to read because it displays the United Methodist Church carrying out the will of a majority of its authoritative General Conference against a faithful and effective minister who sees his pastoral role to be one of inclusive ministry to the people of his congregation, gay and straight. The trial might not make the big history books, but these are not ordinary people. It is a picture of a struggle that is taking place all over this country and the world. These are real people fighting against walls of hostility and striving to bring them down.

The second story is an unbelievably intimate, honest telling of Roller's own personal life, at times so forthright that you feel like a voyeur. The early loss of her father, her family thrown into poverty by his death, the strange unsatisfying character of her first marriage, life with her children, her call to ordained ministry, a time of open marriage, her deep conviction about welcoming gay and lesbian people into the church and the wider public, a fulfilling but all too brief second marriage: All these and more make this a history of real, not ordinary, people, and of one person's journey to faith and life.

The first time I read the manuscript, I told Roller that this was two books, but then as I re-read and worked through it, I came to realize it is one book skillfully connecting two stories that, in fact, are one history. It is the kind of history we need in this important time of struggle over the issue of homosexuality. It is this kind of narrative that tells what is happening down on the ground in the real lives of real people. These are the voices and the stories we must not miss by focusing only on the so-called "big events."

This issue will not be won by kings and queens, by presidents and legislators, or by authoritative church bodies, as important as they might be in some ways; this will be won by real people dealing with the flesh and blood realities of one of the important issues of our time.

INTRODUCTION

My best childhood memories are of my mother reading to my three brothers and me. Something important took root within me during those times and stayed with me throughout my life: the idea that curiosity, wonder and the quest for freedom were essential for a life well lived.

At story time, when it all began, Mother would sit on a chair above us as we gathered around her feet in a little circle on the bare wood floor in the living room of our rented home. Sometimes we dressed in our oldest shorts and T-shirts, other times in our pajamas. Our two older sisters, who didn't want to hear "kids' stories," would flit through the room now and then, but their footsteps were quiet since we all went barefoot at home to help with the Florida heat and to save our shoes, along with our good clothes, for school and church.

Most of the time our widowed mom was working as the secretary of our large downtown church that proclaimed on its letterhead, "In the heart of Tampa for over a century." When she was at home, she was kept so busy cooking, washing clothes and managing the constant chaos we six children created she was too tired to give us much emotional care in her few free moments.

But at story time, ah, she enchanted us by reading with all the dramatic skill she had honed from an earlier job teaching kindergarten children, pouring out upon us the elixir of love and attention we all craved but otherwise rarely received.

Her eyes twinkled and her mouth smiled as she read and turned the book around to show us each illustration. Our little circle was aglow with her energy and love. She was totally there, totally present to us.

She read us all kinds of stories, and even when she had read them many times before, her voice was filled with contagious excitement. I enjoyed every story, but my favorite—the one that would have a lasting impression—was written by Tasha Tudor.

The White Goose tells of a young boy named Robin who is looking for his missing white goose. He calls out for her and hears "that other Robin, the echo of himself, calling from the midst." Suddenly he senses a presence behind him and turns to see a white feather on the ground and, not far from it, another. Following white feathers to the river, he finds many wild geese standing on grass, which is silvery with frost and moonlight. Among them stands a little girl whose lovely laughter echoes across the river. The geese make way as she walks to Robin and takes his hand.

"'Come quickly,' said she. 'It will soon be daylight. Here is a fine gander; jump on his back and fly away with us!'

"'Fly away with us!' echoed the geese."

But Robin hesitates as he thinks about home, his little sister in her cradle and his mother singing in the kitchen. Even though he is invited to see wonderful things, including the other side of the moon, Robin resists.

Tears slip down the little girl's face and she disappears. In her place stands the missing white goose. It lingers for only a moment, then joins the other geese as they rise into the air on thundering wings. Robin is left alone standing in the moonlight.

At the book's conclusion, children are enticed to see things that others say aren't really there, to hear that little girl's laughter and to do what Robin couldn't bring himself to do—to fly up the shaft of moonlight to the hidden side of the moon.

I thought about this story a lot and always with a tinge of sadness. I thought, for instance, about how Robin's beloved goose must have greeted him each time he left the warmth, safety and confines of his house; how, almost unnoticed, she probably tagged along as Robin walked in the fields, rested in the hayloft of the barn and watched the light sparkle on the lake. I imagined how the wonder of the world around him inspired Robin's imagination to run free. But, as beautiful as his dreams were, he chose not to act on them. Thus, he missed the joy of the mysterious journey.

Nonetheless, this story and its beautiful illustrations sparked my imagination and caused delicious shivers to run up and down my body. I wondered how I could fly with the white goose for just one night so I could discover the mysteries Robin was afraid to explore—even as I realized, with a shudder, the courage such a journey would require.

The White Goose eventually became a metaphor for me of the way Spirit works in our lives—at first as quiet companion while we explore our immediate world, but eventually becoming a compelling force that urges us to travel farther and to see clearer while trusting its mysterious, life-giving presence. If we accept and devote ourselves to what always comes as invitation (rather than coercion) from the alternative world Jesus caught sight of and embodied, then ego, familiarity and safety become less important.

Discovering and embracing this world inspired enduring passions that led me to write this book. They are, in fact, what this story is all about.

Passion about the importance of embracing our curiosity and wonder even as the world urges us to fit ourselves into cultural and religious norms—whether or not the fit is logical, wise or meaningful for us.

Passion to show the importance of claiming freedom for ourselves and insisting upon it for others while also insisting that personal freedom be balanced with social responsibility.

And passion to reveal the emotional violence inflicted upon all of us when religious and secular cultures attempt to limit humanity's amazing and beautiful diversity.

Not surprisingly, such enthusiasms led to a good deal of angst. On the one hand, I wanted to embrace these passions while staying within the boundaries of my religious faith—my theological home—due to my appreciation of the multitude of spiritual gifts it offers and my understanding of the need for doctrinal order.

On the other hand, I longed to be swept up by the mysterious and wondrous wind of Ruach, a scriptural name for God represented by the invitation of the little girl. I longed to go to the other side of the moon—a place unseen, unknown and threatening to so much of the world—where all people might truly love and appreciate one another.

Like Robin, I felt the universal agony of having to choose between limiting myself to the safety of the home I knew and loved and finding the courage to go forth to learn and grow. And, like Robin, I hesitated. But, gratefully, the sound of thundering wings was finally too much for me to resist. Thus, I chose, and keep choosing, to spend my life searching for and sometimes flying with the white goose. The stories that follow illustrate my ongoing search and show ways others have responded to the mysterious urgings of God.

Following my passions didn't always lead me to break boundaries or to experience wonderful new worlds, of course. But even the seeking demanded more courage and strength than I ever thought I had. It also required that I learn to have patience when I realized that the freedom I sought for myself and others was still far from reach, or even worse, might not be achieved in my lifetime.

Nonetheless, it became clear to me that when I learned to respectfully listen and carefully attend to the inner voice that is the source of all true passion—when I followed the white feathers—I often had moments of such complete wonder, mystery and joy that I seemed to share a heartbeat with God. And once experienced, there was no going back. The road forward became my home, compelling if not comfortable. Even questions unanswered and quests unrealized could not turn me back. I was changed and my world with me.

I am an ordained United Methodist clergywoman. As you may have already gleaned, along with reverence, I have always had a lover's quarrel with the institutional church for the ways it never fully lives up to its purpose.

Even so, I am grateful for much of its heritage and ministry and especially for bringing me the life and words of Jesus, which sustain me, especially his promise: "I came that all may have life, and have it to the full" (paraphrase of John 10:10b, The Jerusalem Bible). My gratitude for this truth inspires me to want to keep his great commandment: "You must love … God with all your heart, with all your soul and with all your mind…. You must love your neighbor as yourself" (Matthew 22:37–39, The Jerusalem Bible).

I hope this book will illustrate how loving self and others as Jesus did while fully embracing God's gift of life inevitably leads us to mysterious places and difficult choices. Scripture tells us that the wind called Ruach blows wherever it pleases (paraphrase of John 3:8a, The Jerusalem Bible). This drives button-down types crazy, and I'll admit it has been quite disturbing—even agonizing during periods of my life—to discover that God doesn't necessarily respect our rules and regulations, our cultural constructs, our sense of authority and security, or our religious doctrines. That, in fact, if love isn't happening, Ruach is pretty good at bringing us to our knees until we become willing to offer our illusion of security in exchange for reverence to that which is greater than we are and which is never completely knowable.

I have chosen to weave together relevant portions of my personal history with the story of an important church trial. I was not legally involved in the trial story, and the subject it dealt with—homosexuality—was not the central focus of my ministry. Yet this issue has had a considerable impact upon my life, weaving itself inexorably into my own story.

While other socially constricted areas of life have been somewhat freed, this area lags behind in social acceptance, much less social justice. In fact, my denomination, along with many others, seems frightened of the very idea that gays and lesbians might share in the rights and privileges that heterosexuals enjoy, and it is frantic to make sure that they don't.

Through this book, you will have a rare view of how church leaders handle issues about homosexuality behind the scenes. Although some incidents are difficult to write about, I do so in order to add my voice to the growing number of those who seek God's justice, peace, freedom and wholeness for us all.

I have done my best to include all that is essential to the story without elaborating upon certain details or naming some of those involved because to do so might cause unnecessary pain to people I sincerely wish well, including those whom I have caused pain and those who have seriously injured me. I also realize that nothing I can say or do will spare them the consequences of their actions any more than I could escape the consequences of my own choices. Nonetheless, I trust that God's grace is abundant enough for us all.

We can never have too many reminders of what is real and what we can count on. We can never hear enough about how someone survived terrifying tragedies and, thus, gain reassurance that we might survive the ones that come along in our own lives. We must never tire of seeing injustice revealed and finding fresh ways to resist it. And we all need to hear again and again stories of what is beautiful, hopeful and true; stories that remind us of God's love and passionate involvement in our lives; stories that encourage us to keep searching and listening for those thundering wings and embracing the wind called Ruach as it carries us wherever it will.

Ermalou M. Roller

CHAPTER ONE

At 5:00 AM, the sable-colored German Shepherd jumped onto the tarmac from the open back door of the unmarked van, his ears erect. His handler, dressed in khaki, held the dog on a tight leash as the animal looked toward the uniformed police officer standing ten feet away by the side of his patrol car.

"Stay, Cooper!" the handler commanded, then reached down and stroked the animal's head while repeating the mantra familiar and reassuring to both of them. "Good boy, Cooper, good dog."

Cooper looked up at his handler with anticipation, as his breath sent white vapor into the bone-chilling air. Although obviously well trained to follow commands, he looked eager to get to work.

The nearby police officer moved away from his cruiser and walked quickly toward one of the large doors of the church.

"I'll open up. The pastor gave us a key," he called out, trying his best to be nonchalant while glancing nervously at the muscular dog's dark eyes.

"Thanks," the handler said, holding onto the dog's leash while turning to his partner, who had just exited the van after reporting their arrival on the radio.

"I'll handle Coop if you'll grab the scan, Bob," he said.

The second agent, also dressed in khaki, nodded his assent, reached into the back of the vehicle and carefully lifted the 12-pound, battery-powered, Golden X-Ray scanner from its mounting rack.

Just then an early morning jogger veered off of Maple Street, intending to cut through the church parking lot. Startled, he stopped abruptly at the sight of the patrol car, the policeman, the unmarked van and the powerful-looking dog quivering with unspent energy at the end of its master's leash.

He stood for a moment wondering what was going on. Sensing danger, his body tensed as he watched the two agents and the dog quickly disappear after the policeman inside the church. Seeing nothing more, he shrugged his shoulders and resumed his run.

Half a block further, the jogger came to Fishel Park on Grove Street. He stopped once more, this time to stretch his tense legs, and noticed a maintenance crew moving quickly through the large grounds.

Watching the workers pick up the crushed pop cans, discarded chewing gum and candy wrappers while still thinking about the scene at the church, he smiled. It occurred to him that perhaps the litter left every night by teens was the way they claimed this space as their own—at least temporarily—much the way the eager German Shepherd, if given the chance, would mark the corners of the park with his urine to ward off other dogs.

What the jogger didn't know was that today the teens and dogs would have to yield to the out-of-towners, who would mingle there all day and well into this night and the next.

They would be gathering for the church trial that would begin in a few hours a half-block away in the sanctuary of the church he had just passed: First United Methodist Church, the spiritual home for a congregation of 3,000.

Most United Methodists didn't know that church trials could still be conducted, having read of them only in history courses at school, where they were associated primarily with witchcraft. But events within the church had been foreshadowing today's trial for some time.

Several years earlier, when pastors and parishioners had asked the denomination to affirm the sexual orientation and committed relationships of gays and lesbians, it responded by condemning their "lifestyle." Further, it prohibited their unions to take place in United Methodist churches and forbade its pastors from officiating at such unions. At the same time, it patronized the gay, lesbian, bisexual and transgendered (GLBT) community by also declaring in an official publication that, "Homosexual persons no less than heterosexual persons are individuals of sacred worth."

In spite of the edicts, one Chicago area pastor, sympathetic to the damage being inflicted upon his GLBT parishioners, dared to officiate at the same-sex union of two members of his church. He had quietly performed such unions for a decade or more until an outraged colleague found out and brought charges against him.

Now the simmering turmoil surrounding the confusing stand on homosexuality within the entire United Methodist denomination would be thrashed out and clarified at this peaceful suburban village 25 miles west of Chicago. The precedent-setting verdict would soon be reported on all national news broadcasts.

Supporters of the trial's defendant would come to Fishel Park with their guitars, singing voices, placards and prophetic hope to demonstrate their convictions during the strange event. They would include members of the Methodist Federation for Social Action (MFSA) and others desiring to see that the church become inclusive.

However, some people planned to come to the streets proclaiming hell and damnation to homosexuals and all who supported them. Fred Phelps and his Westboro Baptist Church's anti-gay propagandist group, based in Topeka, Kansas, promised to bring 1,000 protesters. These were the same people who had picketed servicemen's funerals as well as churches open to the GLBT community by gathering at these various sites to shout bigoted slogans and carry signs proclaiming that God hates homosexuals.

All of this made the local pastor, the Rev. Fred Conger, nervous. Fearing danger, he asked for the help of the local police. At first the department expressed anger that the community was being subjected to an unnecessary threat due to Conger's willingness to host the trial. Nonetheless, the Downers Grove Police Department joined forces with the DuPage County Bomb Squad to help reduce the risk of violence.

It would take the two agents—one guiding Cooper's highly sensitive and well-educated nose, and the other using the bomb scanner—less than an hour to declare the entire church structure safe. They would repeat their procedures on the morning of the second day of the trial just as efficiently.

Meanwhile, workers continued to gather up litter in Fishel Park across the alley from a cluster of tall gravestones in the cemetery. Each side of the alley silently pleaded, if you will, its own pretrial case. The park litter argued for the messy, exuberant promise of young life on the move; the tall, impressive gravestones pleaded for loyalty to the status quo unto death. The contrast of the two provided the perfect symbol for the crisis the United Methodist Church found itself facing. It could either choose to embrace emerging science and contextual theological interpretation of scripture or remain ensconced in its conservative, literalist tradition. Either choice would make many people unhappy enough to withdraw their church membership.

United Methodists had no inkling of the trial outcome or how they would respond. Perhaps they would be able to celebrate fresh unity in a revitalized, forward-looking church willing to endure the messiness of change. Maybe they would struggle to hang in with a denomination whose rigid doctrine would remain, at best, embarrassing. Or they might join others in withdrawing from a dying organization that refused to share God's good news with everyone.

I was a romantic—one of those hoping for, if not expecting, a miracle. I had worked for my denomination's complete acceptance of gays and lesbians for years as a clergywoman. It made no sense to me that people could personally accept God's unconditional love, then try to build some kind of barrier to prevent others from doing the same. Clearly such an exclusive attitude did not reflect what Jesus told us, how he lived or why he died.

I identified with the brokenness of those outside the theological fence, due to past times in my life that had been fraught with personal pain heightened by the negative judgments and assumptions of significant others in my life, including those in the church. Having been an outsider myself, I became less judgmental of others. At the same time, I became suspicious of and increasingly impatient with excessive religious certitude, especially when it hurt and attempted to exclude people from God's circle of love.

As a mother, I felt concern about the pain the impending trial would inflict upon my beloved 37-year-old son, Stan. Only one year before, he had told me that he was gay—something I had long suspected. An articulate man with a handsome face and a sharp intelligence, Stan worked for a Big Six accounting firm in Chicago. Disillusioned by our denominational stand on his sexual orientation, he withdrew his membership. I urged him many times to try once more at Broadway United Methodist in Chicago where the pastor, the Rev. Gregory Dell, had created a safe and inclusive community that included but not was not exclusive to gays and lesbians. I knew that Stan would be welcomed there. He listened politely but did nothing.

Then he saw an article about Greg in a local newspaper regarding the growing controversy that would eventually lead to the trial. He marveled at the congregational support the pastor enjoyed after being challenged about his practice of officiating at same-sex unions.

The colleague who brought the complaint claimed Greg had broken new church law and demanded that he be charged with unprofessional and unfaithful conduct. However, most if not all of Greg's congregants felt that his willingness to conduct same-sex unions was as faithful a pastoral act as when he officiated at heterosexual marriages. They pledged to stand with him no matter what happened.

Impressed, Stan figured that since the Broadway congregation was willing to go so far to defend their beliefs, "It was time for me to put up or shut up," he told me. "That's what got me out of my apartment and there on Sunday morning."

He felt moved by the worship service, and especially by the powerful choir. He had forgotten how much all this meant to him. But as he continued to worship there, the most important thing he experienced was the joy of being fully accepted by a community of faith.

"Mom, the Broadway congregation doesn't just welcome and tolerate me," he said. "They actually celebrate who I am. I've never had that kind of affirmation before, and I like it!" He quickly became an involved member.

As the controversy grew, so did Stan's excitement. He kept me updated in our weekly phone conversations.

"It's a heady experience being here, Mom. I feel like something very big is about to happen—something that's going to make a real difference, something I'm glad to be part of. It's really something to wake up in the morning and see a story about my church on the front page of the *Chicago Tribune*. I mean, it isn't some mega church. There are only about 150 of us."

Around that time, he flew to Tampa on business and stopped in a bar, where he read *This Week Magazine* (*TWM*, a gay rag, which primarily features information about regional events). Twelve-hundred miles from Chicago and surprised to see an article about Broadway UMC, Stan proudly said to the guy next to him, "I'm a member of that church!"

The Sunday before the trial began he told me how excited he felt stepping off the Broadway bus and seeing CNN and every other major news van parked in front of the church with their large antennas and wiring draped everywhere.

"Inside, we were given tips about media relations," he said, "like what your options are when someone sticks a microphone in your face as you leave the worship service. Of course, some gay and lesbian people aren't ready to 'come out' yet to their friends and family, much less to the nation. So they were given instructions on how to avoid reporters."

Listening to his stories and hearing his joy about being part of making a difference in our world, I felt thrilled that a group of diverse people with big hearts and open minds had helped Stan reconnect to a worshipping community. His spirit had taken root once more and begun to flourish.

At that time, I was serving in my third local church appointment as senior pastor of St. Andrew United Methodist Church in Homewood, Illinois. I was enjoying my fifth joyful and satisfying year. My husband had just retired, and we were taking pleasure in having more time for one another. We felt grateful to be part of the vibrant community of friendly, spirit-seeking, committed people.

Only 20 years old, our lovely sanctuary featured congregational seating arranged in a half circle surrounded by stunning contemporary stained-glass windows set in a brick background. An imaginative master craftsman had designed and built the dais furniture. A large gathering area, adjacent to the worship area, provided space where people could linger and talk before and after worship services. The outstanding music program included multiple voice and bell choirs.

My congregation was well educated and savvy enough to attract good preachers. They had enjoyed outstanding leadership for many years and intended for that to continue. The average attendance on Sunday mornings was 145.

Up to this point, I had loved almost everything about the United Methodist Church. It had been my denominational home since childhood. I felt grateful to serve it for many years as an adult. But due to the denomination's recent doctrinal changes regarding homosexuals and a growing awareness of the fragility of my romantic hope for those positions shifting, I began to realize that my love for it was being replaced by anger, even shame.

In a very real way I, and others like me, felt as much on trial as Greg. We had struggled for more inclusiveness in this church for years; now the same church threatened to invalidate our ministry. Further, my family's life had been deeply harmed by negative views of homosexuals. If the trial verdict supported such views, many other families would also suffer unnecessarily.

How did the church ever get here? And how did I ever get to this place?

summer, 1974
naperville · illinois

No one, including me, would have ever guessed that I was headed for disaster at the age of 35. I fit the description of a typical Christian, Anglo-American, Midwestern, suburban housewife with three young children at home and a husband busy building an impressive career. We lived in a comfortable split-level home in a neighborhood with shady trees and sidewalks. I volunteered at our church.

Eventually I would realize that much of my life was cruel illusion, when comfortable, predictable normality became replaced with devastating shame, pain and confusion. I should have seen the crisis coming, but my good-girl naiveté overweighed the obvious for a long, long time.

Fifteen years earlier, I first began noticing Gary, who was

slender and handsome with thick, dark brown hair and lively brown eyes. I learned that he had graduated with honors from the University of Florida with a bachelor's degree in building construction and was working for a building supply company in town. I had graduated from Hillsborough High School and was attending the University of Tampa, majoring in education. I paid for my classes by working part-time as a secretary for Robert T. Mann, a state legislator and partner in a law firm.

My growing interest in Gary inspired a question for my mother, "How will I know when I am in love?"

She answered, "You'll just know."

That confused me about how to label what I felt for Gary. I knew he was a talented, hardworking, nice man, and I did feel attracted to him. I enjoyed his company and thought he was someone I could live with. Plus, the cultural norm at the time dictated that a girl be at least engaged by the time she was 19 (my age) or risk being labeled an "old maid." I was feeling the pressure, so I quickly accepted when Gary asked me for a date.

About six months after we began seeing one another, Mother decided to invite Gary and his parents to dinner at our home to become better acquainted. There would be only five of us since my sisters and brothers were all living on their own.

We rarely entertained, and Mom and I felt anxious about how the worn sofa and bare floors reflected our poverty. Gary and his parents lived in a large home with rugs on the floor of a large living room and separate dining room. Screened porches graced the front, side and back of the house. His father owned an auto repair business and earned enough money to allow his mother to be a full-time homemaker. She kept their house clean and served them well-prepared meals with home-baked desserts. Although we had done our best to straighten up, Mom and I knew our guests couldn't help but notice the difference in our standard of living. She talked to me about this ahead of time.

"We can be proud of what we've accomplished and who we are, Ermalou," she told me, her right forefinger touching her lips in a familiar, anxious gesture. "We are going to hold our heads up high," she added forcefully. I realized that she was feeling as vulnerable as I was.

The white ruffled curtains laundered especially for this occasion were blowing in a gentle breeze when our guests arrived.

The five of us enjoyed a good, simple meal: beef stew with potatoes and carrots, summer squash with onions, Cuban bread, a pickle and olive tray, and ice cream for dessert. After dinner we helped Mom clear the table and, at her insistence, left the dishes for her to hand-wash later.

"Let's just sit and talk," she said.

I felt relieved that we women didn't have to gather in the tiny, disorganized kitchen with our everyday glasses—chipped jelly jars—showing on the open shelves.

We walked to the other end of the open space that served as living room and dining room to sit down. After a few minutes of polite conversation, Gary stood up, walked to where I was sitting, and got down on one knee in front of me.

"Ermalou," he said, "I've wanted to ask you this for a long time. Will you marry me?"

I felt surprised and extremely embarrassed. *Isn't this supposed to be romantic?* I thought. *Isn't this usually something private between a man and woman? Why is he doing this here and now?*

Without waiting for my answer, he pulled a small, black velvet box from the pocket of his trousers and opened it up for me to see. Inside was the beautiful engagement ring that I had loved when we casually looked at rings together—as if flirting with the unspoken idea of marriage. It was a simple, contemporary creation with four raised rays of silver on top and was designed so the sparkling half-carat diamond in the center looked like a beautiful star.

Still embarrassed that he was doing this in front of our parents, yet thrilled with the proposal, I quickly said, "Yes." He slipped the ring onto my finger, stood and pulled me up, leading me to where his parents sat.

"Isn't this beautiful?" he asked them.

He extended my ring finger closer to them. I forced a smile and cooperated by turning my hand back and forth, allowing them to carefully inspect the ring.

"This is the newest design. See these silver rays?" Gary gushed. "The wedding ring has a notch on one side, and it'll slip into one of the rays so that the two rings hold together. And look at the size of that diamond! It's really gorgeous, isn't it?"

His father responded with an appreciative murmur. His mother praised him.

"This is the prettiest ring I've ever seen. You've done a magnificent job, son. Ermalou is a lucky girl to wear this on her finger."

We walked over to my mother. I could tell that she shared my discomfort.

"Yes, it's lovely," she said while giving me a knowing look. "I think Gary is lucky to have Ermalou wear it!"

It was impossible not to notice that Gary was more interested in our parents' admiration of his ring choice than in having a private moment with me. But questioning him later seemed pointless and ungrateful. I remained disappointed yet determined not to make a big deal out of it and let it ruin the moment. However, instead of dissipating, my confusion would continue to grow as our relationship developed.

After a two-year engagement, Gary and I were married on June 10, 1961, at First Methodist Church in Tampa, a week after my graduation from Florida State University. Mother made me a full-length gown featuring lace embossed over organza with hand-sewn seed pearls. My brother Edward "gave me away," and my other four siblings were included among the eight attendants.

Our Nassau honeymoon felt delightful in many ways. We rode about in a horse-pulled carriage, swam in the clear warm water, sunbathed on the beach and enjoyed the nightlife. However, our first night together proved to be confusing and disappointing.

We arrived on the island at sunset. After a late dinner we returned to our room.

"Let's get ready for bed," Gary said.

Feeling embarrassed to prepare for the culmination of our glorious wedding day in front of my groom, I changed in the tiny bathroom while willing myself to have courage. I put on the sheer white nightgown with matching negligee that Mother and I had taken weeks of shopping to find and slipped my feet into my new satin slippers. Having always worn pajamas to bed before this supremely romantic moment, I felt both excited and a bit like a counterfeit princess. I combed my hair just right and brushed my teeth for an extra long time to ensure that my breath smelled sweet. Finally I opened the door and shyly presented myself to Gary.

He gave me a quick glance and said, "Why don't you just take that thing off?"

I felt shocked and keenly disappointed. I had expected to hear him say that I looked beautiful. I had hoped he would admire my body and put me at ease. Swallowing my humiliation, I did as he asked.

"Come lie down," he said, patting the bed next to where he was lying naked.

When I did, he quickly ended my virginity without tenderness or foreplay. His body felt heavy and abusive. I cried out in pain and felt shocked again when he responded with indifference. When he rolled over with his back facing me to go to sleep, I felt unbearably lonely and confused.

Fifteen years later the confusion and loneliness continued, and I still had no idea what to do about it.

CHAPTER TWO

The church's journey to the Dell trial was full of irony. In the United Methodist denomination, a church trial is required when a charge is brought against a pastor and the matter cannot be resolved through negotiations with the presiding bishop and the involved parties.

The controversial pastoral/administrative leader of the Northern Illinois Conference of the United Methodist Church was Bishop C. Joseph Sprague, an eloquent, spiritually grounded, courageous and unstoppable force for justice. Bishop Sprague had officiated at several homosexual covenant services earlier in his ministry (when this was not against church law), but now found himself unable to resolve a charge brought against one of his pastors for doing the same (after the new church law prohibited such action).

At that point, he had two options, one of which included the possibility of arranging for a trial to be conducted against the Rev. Gregory R. Dell, whom he later described as "an exemplary pastor whose record of faithfulness is, in my opinion, beyond reproach."

Sprague's referral was made in response to the charge of a colleague who claimed that Dell had violated his sacred trust as a pastor. This complaint had been duly examined by the official body named the Committee on Investigation. They found that the complaint was made on reasonable grounds. The bishop struggled with whether to handle it as an Administrative Complaint, with the possibility of referring it to the conference Board of Ordained

Ministry for final resolution, or deal with it as a Judicial Complaint, which would result in a trial.

As he considered his options, Bishop Sprague was acutely aware of the recent history of litigation around this issue. Another United Methodist clergyman, the Rev. Jimmy Creech, had been brought to trial for officiating at a union service just a year before.

That trial had taken place in 1997, one year after our denomination added a unique statement to the Social Principles section of *The Book of Discipline of the United Methodist Church*. This book contains the denomination's constitution, history, doctrinal statements, general rules and social principles.

The added portion stated that clergy and churches must not be involved in homosexual union ceremonies. This 1996 addition was unique because it could be interpreted as law about clergy conduct in a section of our *Discipline* usually reserved for expressions of social beliefs that are intended to be instructive and persuasive.

The change was made at the General Conference, a meeting of elected United Methodist delegates from annual conferences around the world. Held every four years, this conference functions as our only legislative body. There the delegates talk with each other about important, often controversial social issues including but not limited to abortion, war, rights of children, alcohol/drugs and sexuality. Eventually they adopt position statements for the church, which become part of the Social Principles. Everyone understands these statements might be revised in ensuing years as new information emerges and/or hearts change. Because of their nature, statements in the Social Principles are considered by many if not most pastors as suggestive rather than binding.

The law of the church, found in another section of the *Discipline*, is another matter. Like civil law, church law is subject to interpretation and change. But rather than being "instructive and persuasive," it requires adherence and spells out the consequences of noncompliance. This is especially true for clergy who promise to uphold the "order and discipline" of the church.

The swirl of controversy around the action the Rev. Jimmy Creech no doubt focused the determination of those who interpreted the new Social Principles statement as church law. On September 17 of that year, Creech performed a holy union service for two women at the First UMC in Omaha, Nebraska, where he served as senior pastor. As a result, on November 10, he was suspended for 60 days by his bishop, Joel N. Martinez. By January 23, 1998, the Committee on Investigation of the Nebraska UM Annual Conference (the gathering of that regional group) found the charge against him valid and called for a church trial.

Retired Bishop Leroy C. Hodapp presided at that trial from March 11–13. Creech was acquitted by a one-vote margin and reinstated as senior pastor of First UMC in Omaha. Nonetheless, on May 6, Martinez refused to reappoint Creech for the next year, saying that he had failed to bring healing to the congregation. Creech then took a leave of absence from ministry.

In 1998 the Judicial Council, the highest judicial body of the United Methodist Church, reviewed the new addition to the Social Principles and declared that it was law. This drew a line in the sand for all clergy who disagreed with the ruling: Either adhere to the new church law or suffer severe consequences.

As a result, just two days before the Dell trial, Bishop Melvin G. Talbert of the San Francisco area, who is supportive of gay and lesbian rights, reluctantly filed a complaint against 68 pastors in Sacramento, California, for their role in co-officiating at a holy union service there. (They would come to be known as the "Sacramento 68.") A total of 1,500 guests, including 92 United Methodist pastors, had been present and participated in the service, but 24 of those clergy served outside of the jurisdiction of the California–Northern Nevada Conference and so were not named in the formal complaint.

This complaint, however, was never brought to trial. The official reason given was that the charges were not serious enough to warrant such action. The real reasons probably included the cost of such a proceeding, plus the fact that if the clergy were found guilty, churches would be left without pastoral leadership.

I joined with many other United Methodists in applauding the courage and skillful strategy of the Sacramento 68 and enjoyed a good laugh at how they had audaciously skirted the system for the sake of justice.

But this laughter was soon replaced by apprehension when the Dell controversy emerged in the Northern Illinois Conference. Along with being troubled about my son, I felt concern for Greg, a treasured colleague. Even before I entered seminary I had heard about Greg's excellent ministry as a student associate at the church just kitty-corner from the one I attended in Naperville, Illinois. He and his wife, Jade, were instrumental in the success of a cooperative nonprofit childcare service I had formed with others in 1973.

They brought their young son, Jason, to the Mother's Day Out program, and for several weeks he was the only child there. But the word got out and soon we had to place 25 new applicants on a waiting list. We might have folded without Greg and Jade's support but now, partly because of it, this program (sporting the more inclusive name of Kid's Day Out) is still available and serving that community nearly 40 years later.

After my ordination, I served with Greg on an important board of the conference. I often heard him speak from the floor at our annual conferences and appreciated his passionate quest to bring hope to all people our society leaves behind. If he were defrocked, we would lose an effective pastor as well as an important and passionate voice for justice.

I worried about some of my parishioners who were already suffering from our denomination's attitude toward their sexual orientation. They would be devastated should Greg be convicted and punished for effectively ministering to people like themselves. So much damage had already been done to them.

In 1977, for instance, the year I was ordained an elder in the church, former Miss America runner-up and orange juice pitchwoman, Anita Bryant, used her prominence to speak out against a progressive gay rights ordinance in Dade County, Florida, resulting in its repeal.

Another tragic event happened in 1978, when gay activist Harvey Milk was murdered at City Hall, along with Mayor George Moscone, 11 months after being elected to San Francisco's board of supervisors. Having received many death threats, Milk often spoke of his possible assassination, even recording a will with the line, "If a bullet should enter my brain, let that bullet destroy every closet door."

Fear joined hatred in 1981, when cases of Pneumocystis carinii pneumonia (PCP, a lung infection) and Kaposi's sarcoma (a rare skin cancer) were reported by doctors in New York and Los Angeles. Initially these infections were called "gay cancer," then they acquired the designation GRID (Gay-Related Immune Deficiency). Scientists later found that the disease had existed in the world for some years in Africa and was likely transmitted from humans eating infected chimpanzees. Cases began to be reported in 14 nations.

Meanwhile, the Centers for Disease Control and Protection began tracking a growing population of young men, women and babies whose immune systems were nearly destroyed. In 1983, a French doctor (Luc Montagnier of the Pasteur Institute) announced the isolation of the virus that was later identified as the cause of AIDS (Acquired Immune Deficiency Syndrome).

That same year, when more than 300 people had died and 800 had become infected, the mainstream media response to the frightening disease remained lethargic. Even after researchers discovered the AIDS virus, the *New York Times* refused to cover an April organizational fundraiser for Gay Men's Health Crisis (GMHC). Fortunately, the AP and UPI did feed the story to newspapers in other cities, and television stations featured the story of how 11,000 concerned well-wishers had filled Madison Square Garden.

I felt grateful that ten years before, in 1973, the United Methodist Church had joined with Lutheran, Presbyterian and Quaker denominations to launch the National Task Force on Gay People in the Church, which was recognized by the governing board of the National Council of Churches. This seemed to be an effort to understand homosexuals and to find ways to offer them God's justice and grace.

Now I reeled with disappointment that my denomination seemed headed toward withdrawing from some people the very thing we all need most, the gift of grace Jesus brought into the world, that unconditional love of God for all people everywhere. I wasn't sure I could continue to be part of a denomination that refused to honor God's commandment that we love our neighbors as ourselves.

1957
tampa · florida

My first two years of college were spent at the University of Tampa. Every afternoon I walked across the Lafayette Street Bridge over the Hillsborough River to downtown Tampa and Bob Mann's law firm (Graham & Mann), where I worked as his secretary in order to pay for my tuition and books.

Eventually I followed Bob's advice to transfer to Florida State University, where I finished my studies. He helped me secure a part-time job at a capital office building in downtown Tallahassee. I was glad to be working for those administering the new National Defense Education Act. It provided funds to aid school education and addressed institutional sexism, insisting that funds be used for girls' programs as well as those for boys.

Gary wrote to me every day. I felt grateful for his patience about my long absences. He encouraged me to complete my degree work in spite of his mother's attitude. She thought I should quit school if I really loved him because, she said, "Women don't need an education." My father's death had convinced me otherwise.

In 1940, my father died suddenly at work at the age of 37, leaving Mom, my two sisters, three brothers and me to survive on our own. Dad's coworker reported looking up from his desk and noticing that "Mac" had grown very pale. Concerned, he stood and began walking toward him when Dad collapsed onto the floor and could not be revived. He was pronounced dead on arrival at the hospital.

We children were all thrust into emotional chaos, too young to really understand what had happened or how to deal with our individual and collective panic. Joan was ten years old. I was ten months. The rest of my siblings—Clarice, Cliff, John and Edward—were a year or two apart.

I remember nothing of this time and have no memories of my dad. Yet in retrospect, I believe that this event shaped my life in a profound way.

Obviously, I wouldn't have understood why Dad wasn't at breakfast the next morning, why he permanently disappeared, and why Mom suddenly left me with the neighbor next door for most of each day. I'm told that my brothers and sisters also disappeared, having been sent to live with relatives for the summer while Mom looked for a job.

I promptly developed double pneumonia and was hospitalized and placed in an oxygen tent. Mother felt frantic, fearing that unexpressed grief would kill me, and I think it nearly did. Perhaps the desperate love I saw in Mother's eyes helped me to heal.

I can't help but surmise that my father's death and the

temporary disappearance of the rest of my family created a fear of abandonment that has haunted me for many years. It also must have marked me as different by separating me from the life experience of other neighborhood children. Whatever the cause, I began a long process of sympathizing with those who found themselves unable to identify with "normal" American life.

Not having the luxury of falling apart after Dad's death, Mom assumed a stoic stance that she never fully relinquished in the ensuing years. Unfortunately, this contributed to her reluctance to share much about our father with us. I felt increasingly confused and wondered what this meant about their relationship as well as what it felt like to have a man in the house.

I longed to hear stories about Dad, to be given imaginative tools through Mother's memories to experience his love, which I desperately needed. But when asked to reveal more about him, she often deferred, saying, "Oh, that seems like such a long time ago, another lifetime."

One of the very few anecdotes she did share—although a source of guilt and sadness to her—became an emotional touchstone for me. Even though I remember nothing about the interaction, I savored the mental images her story evoked and freely embellished them to meet my needs.

As a ten-month-old baby, she told me, I was full of curious energy. My dad's adoration was animated and consistent. On the day he died I awoke to the sound of my parents' voices in the next room. They were having an early breakfast, hoping for some private time before my five siblings and I woke up. When I started chattering, my mom carried me to the breakfast nook. She smiled at my dad, realizing I'd discovered a way to get individual time with him. He reached out his arms to me.

"Well, hello, hello, hello!" he said, holding me above his head and planting the first kiss of the day on my forehead. He was a handsome, slender man with a chiseled face. Thick dark eyebrows arched over blue eyes, and his wide smile revealed deep dimples.

He placed his baby girl in his lap and snuggled me against his chest, kissing me once more on one of my fat cheeks. I kicked my legs with delight and began to move in a way that inspired my first nickname of Squirmy.

He reached around me to finish his cereal while I impulsively stuck my hands in the cold milk and lifted my fingers to my mouth. Drops of milk dripped onto my exposed tummy. I kicked my legs and squealed with surprise. Both parents giggled with me, energized by the freshness of my uninhibited reaction.

Then it was time for him to go. There was something intense and unfinished in the air, but no time to complete it. He stood, kissing me again as he handed me to my mom and gave her a peck on the cheek. Then he left. My mom sighed as she watched him go, the screen door banging behind him. Later that day she would hear the news. Their conversation would always remain unfinished, my search to fill the void of his adoring affection would begin and, rather than end in marriage to Gary, would actually intensify.

In the first decade of our marriage, Gary's approach to lovemaking remained regular but devoid of shared passion. In a rather mechanical way he took care of me and I cared for him. I largely accepted this in the bedroom yet longed daily for the kind of sensitive, affectionate, playful touch I had been told that Dad had given me. In short, I wanted to feel adored again. I carefully followed the advice given in women's magazines to make myself more desirable to my husband, and occasionally I asked for a romantic weekend away. Gary never was interested.

Once, while lying in bed, he expressed confusion. "I just don't get it," he said. "What's all the fuss about women's breasts? I can't see how they are at all exciting. They're just designed to feed newborns, aren't they?"

I agreed. I didn't have a clue.

Years flew by. I taught school, financed a second degree for Gary, gave birth to three children and moved three times. These were largely happy, productive and busy times of acquiring new skills and observing the traditions of areas of the country that were unfamiliar to me. In 1971 we purchased a split-level home in Naperville, Illinois, and settled into suburban life. I enjoyed being fully present to my delightful children while learning about life in the Midwest.

Finally, I had time to catch my breath, and I was surprised to find myself restless. I had been the good girl, the supportive wife and the adoring mother. So why wasn't I content?

I felt starved for intellectual stimulation but didn't know how to name that need. I had largely drifted through school, so it didn't occur to me that I wanted to grow mentally. Nonetheless, I found satisfaction getting up in the middle of the night and reading a weekly news magazine. Concepts the journalists presented often challenged me to expand my understanding of the world and its people, and some words were unfamiliar to me, so I kept a dictionary nearby to satisfy my curiosity.

Around this time I also began to realize I was starved for respectful, tender, loving appreciation as a woman. At the time I didn't know how to name that need any more than I knew how to name the intellectual one. I did know how bothered I felt about the way my husband related to me. His actions individually weren't earth shattering but were beginning to add up to my growing discomfort.

I felt unhappy with the way Gary controlled our family finances. He had ready justifications for reasons to spend money on his own needs, those of our sons and for our house, but he always offered excuses as to why meeting our daughter's needs and mine had to be postponed. He walked ahead instead of with me. He refused to shut our bedroom door at night. He patronizingly explained obvious things to me in front of guests and responded to any request I expressed by starting his sentence with, "No…"

This was especially hard to take when he expressed strong opinions about child rearing because I had been the one to earn a degree in childhood education and had some teaching experience. However, my objections to his passionate opinions didn't faze him; when challenged, he simply increased his volume. This became intolerable until I assigned each opinion and its justifications a number in my head. It provided a little private levity to think, "Now I'm going to hear comment #46" and then zone out.

I was unprepared to recognize how serious this was and see the danger that a dominating spouse presents to one's self-esteem. Nor did I feel bold enough to effectively challenge the prevailing values about women in order to hold my own or to claim a new life for myself.

It didn't occur to me, given what had happened to my mother, to question the assumption that the world didn't always reward a woman for following cultural expectations. Nor did I allow the joy and satisfaction Mom had found in her professional work to help me assess and plan my future. I figured that Mom had been the exception to the rule, that other women were happy and fulfilled staying within the exclusive roles of wife, mother and homemaker. Besides, Mother seemed so proud that I was fulfilling the role she hadn't been able to realize. Like a child, I assumed that my feelings meant that something was wrong with me.

CHAPTER THREE

The United Methodist Church's stance on homosexuality essentially began with Thomas Aquinas. Jesus never spoke about homosexuality. However, in Romans 1:26–27a (NRSV), Paul (a major interpreter of Jesus' life and teachings and an influential builder of the early church) writes, "Their women exchanged natural intercourse for unnatural, and in the same way also the men, giving up natural intercourse with women, were consumed with passion for one another."

This solidifies the certitude of some who insist that homosexual orientation is not a natural part of the creation. They also quote other vague references elsewhere in the Bible to support this stance. Therefore, when reading scripture, one has to make several choices: to accommodate or reject current scientific thought, to accept or dismiss the relevance of context, and to decide whom to listen to about this matter—Paul, others who wrote under his name or Jesus, for whom sexual orientation was apparently a non-issue.

Saint Augustine (354–430 AD) superseded Paul by formulating the view that *all* sex is sinful but may be engaged in for reproduction purposes as a kind of necessary evil to sustain human life. He also said sex without reproductive purpose is an unforgivable sin.

Later still, the Christian church in Western Europe avoided Augustine's prudish, even callous stance by largely tolerating or ignoring pronouncements about sexuality until the early part of the Middle Ages (around 1150 AD onward). Then it suddenly demonized gays (along with women, "witches," Jews and Muslims).

At that point Aquinas reasserted Augustine's earlier pronouncements that all non-procreative sexual behavior was sin. His declarations about this and other subjects were likely a response to the church's quest for a solid intellectual base in the face of challenges of heresies within and the increased contact with classical Greek thinkers.

The Roman church had been scandalized, for instance, by Aristotle's philosophy, which focused on physics, metaphysics and the eternity of matter and essentially presented a complete explanation of reality without any reference to a personal God.

Suddenly, the church felt called on to defend its (literal) understanding of the biblical story of creation in order to reestablish its considerable power and leadership over the masses. So it countered Aristotle's ideas with this question: What is it that points to the ultimate reality of our lives, and what shall guide and govern our behavior—reason or theology? The answer for the Roman church was, of course, theology.

The shock for Rome of Aristotle's ideas, which made their way there via Muslims in Spain, can be compared with the 19th-century impact of Darwin's work on North America, when his theory of evolution once again challenged biblical literalism regarding human creation.

While Aristotle's challenge to biblical literalism was still fresh, Aquinas sought to strengthen the church's response by creating his theology of "natural order." Natural order, he said, points to God, is available to all "men" (he meant men literally) and can be studied by reason (philosophy). However, he continued, there is also a supernatural order (theology) that is available through revelation and logical deduction from revelation. This, he insisted, is something only clergy are equipped to do.

The place of sexuality in this philosophy would eventually evolve so that "sin against nature" referred only to homosexual sex when, in fact, it originally meant sex without the aim of fertilizing an egg.

A grateful Roman church eventually accepted Aquinas' ideas and used them to reassert the church's power and leadership. In fact, Aquinas' natural order theory eventually became the primary philosophical approach of the Roman Catholic Church, and many Catholics still consider him to be the church's greatest theologian.

Aquinas was pronounced a saint in 1323. As late as 1879, Pope Leo XIII stated that Aquinas' theology was a definitive exposition of the Catholic doctrine. He directed the clergy to take Aquinas' teachings as the basis of their own theological positions. Further, this pope decreed that all Catholic seminaries and universities must teach Aquinas' doctrines.

Yet Aquinas made a number of theological pronouncements that seem outrageous to most North Americans today. For instance, along with his conviction that the only purpose for sensual and/or sexual activity is procreation, he claimed that the very nature of a woman is defective and misbegotten. Further, he said that anyone who disagreed with or questioned the teachings of the church was a heretic and should be put to death. At the time, the threat of capital punishment effectively curtailed most public criticism, but the excesses and corruption of the Roman church eventually led to the Protestant Reformation.

I hasten to say that theological positions, creeds and rules develop for a variety of reasons, many of which are good: They offer order and safety, or at least an illusion of safety to the faint-hearted; they give language to the inexpressible, offering an inadequate but helpful semblance of clarity to the believer; they create community among people of various backgrounds, intellect, experience and belief; and they educate by sharing the experience of others, illuminating our own possibilities and showing us the consequences of certain choices. Unfortunately, they also often validate the status quo, supporting those in power to continue their domination (whether such domination is deliberate or unintentional).

For these and perhaps other reasons, religious creeds and rules can harm as well as help. Humanity likes to create order—it must do so to create any kind of peace and productivity. Unfortunately, however, we often mistake our theological positions, creeds and rules, all of which are subject to our own limitations and corruptions, for ultimate truth.

When religious ideas become codified, changing them becomes difficult and usually takes a long time. While various individuals are credited with having the courage, intelligence and perseverance to affect such change over the centuries, their actions are usually a kind of flashpoint representing dissatisfaction that has been growing among the populace long enough to reach a critical mass. When this mass is reached, people are ready to listen to and follow the ideas of a reformer.

Martin Luther (1483–1546) is a representative of this phenomenon. For example, when he protested the use of indulgences by the Roman Catholic Church (the practice of charging people for their confessed sins without having to express contrition or do any penance), he touched a raw nerve.

As an Augustinian monk, he wanted only for the church to return to its roots by proclaiming that we are saved by grace and faith (not by our works, including increasing the coffers of the church), but he failed to account for the fact that indulgences had become big business. After nailing his 95 Theses (theologically based protests about indulgences, etc.) to the door of a church, he was found guilty of blasphemy. He escaped punishment by fleeing and hiding out for years. But this flashpoint moment shook the church deeply, eventually dividing it into two camps: Protestant and Roman Catholic.

My denomination has engaged in its own evolutionary

struggles. For instance, Methodist founder John Wesley (1703–1791) was a passionate opponent of slavery. But at the time of its founding, our church, like our country (which had not yet fought the Civil War), was far from ready to agree to the abolishment of slavery. Acrimonious debates between opposing factions ultimately split Methodism into separate northern and southern churches.

Other splits would follow until 1939, when a plan of union brought some of these churches back together by partitioning the united church into six administrative units called jurisdictions. Five of these were geographical. The sixth was racial: the Central Jurisdiction, which included African-American churches and annual conferences wherever they were geographically located in the United States. This shameful arrangement of segregating black people was not corrected until 1968.

Another disgraceful practice was the denial of a place in church leadership for women. Anna Howard Shaw was the first woman ordained in the Methodist tradition in 1880, yet full clergy rights for women, finally granted in 1956, were difficult to achieve and followed long struggles to even have women elected as delegates to our conferences. Our first woman bishop, Marjorie Swank Matthews, was finally elected in 1980, a full century after Shaw's ordination.

The evolving positions reached through ongoing discussion of other theological differences such as war, abortion, nuclear power and peace keep the United Methodist Church's mission statement a working document.

Following the Protestant Reformation, philosophers such as John Locke and scientists such as Copernicus and Galileo moved us to the period called the Enlightenment with watershed developments in science and rational thought. A plethora of biblical scholars kept up with ideas that challenged long-held scriptural understandings. Current scholars such as John Dominick

Crosson (Roman Catholic), John Shelby Spong and Marcus Borg (Episcopalian), Hal Taussig (United Methodist), Walter Wink (Quaker), Karen Armstrong (a former nun) and others continue to offer fresh, progressive interpretation of scripture. But in the spring of 1998, the view of an evolving scriptural interpretation was about to be publicly challenged.

spring, 1998
chicago · illinois

Bishop Sprague tried his best to resolve the Dell conflict without having to go to trial. Neither side was willing to compromise while meeting face to face. He tried once more in a meeting he convened with Rev. Deborah L. Fisher, the Cabinet Dean, Dell and himself. Dell, who by church law had the right to be accompanied by a clergyperson in full connection, brought his good friend, the Rev. Donald F. Guest.

The bishop scheduled the meeting early on a weekday afternoon to be held at the tall Gothic building often referred to as the Chicago Temple, the home of the First United Methodist Church of Chicago. The church and part of the conference offices are housed in the downtown skyscraper along with a number of businesses, mostly law firms that rent space there. This sacred landmark is right across the street from the Richard J. Daley Center, which houses Cook County courtrooms and judges' offices.

The present Chicago Temple structure, the fifth since the church began in a log cabin, was dedicated in 1924, while construction for the Daley Center was not completed until 1965. So although it wasn't planned, it is, nonetheless, an interesting juxtaposition of building locations given Chicago's sullied political reputation. It is also an inadvertent but in-your-face reminder of the denomination's historic insistence that social justice be as vital to the law as personal piety is to the lives of individuals.

Dell and Guest rode into the city together for the meeting.

Arriving on the 18th floor of the skyscraper, reserved exclusively for conference offices, they exited the elevator through its ornate iron doors and went directly to the large meeting room. They found the cabinet dean and the bishop waiting for them at the long, highly polished wooden table. Except for the beige plastic swivel chairs, it was the only piece of furniture in the room. Bishop Sprague and Rev. Fisher rose to greet them, and they all sat down together—a forlorn, sad-looking little group in such a large meeting space.

Dell's intelligent face was sober. Dressed in his usual attire, a sports shirt and slacks, he sat expectant and erect in his revolving chair, prepared to deal with his colleagues with his customary candor and conviction.

Bishop Sprague, emanating gracious empathy, sat across the table, alert and ready to model his philosophy of the importance of having "a tough mind and a tender heart."

Fisher sat next to the bishop, exuding her usual sense of no-nonsense competence. Appreciated for her conference leadership in tackling tough social justice issues, her ready laughter—often a good social bridge—wouldn't be available much this day.

Guest also reflected the subdued tone of the meeting. Knowing that he would add cogent discussion points, Dell felt comforted by his supportive presence.

Along the west wall, large undraped windows revealed a stark scene of brick office buildings and a pale blue, cloudless sky above. Ever-present city pigeons swirled in air currents and cooed on the concrete window ledge outside, sometimes standing on their own droppings. The four colleagues settled in around the table, placing their briefcases in adjoining chairs. Everyone understood that this meeting was required by church law.

Fisher opened the meeting with prayer, asking for God's grace, guidance and justice. Sprague, in the informal, positive style he prefers to use when he can, invited discussion of how to respond to the serious situation at hand. He listened attentively. Finally, he dealt with the bottom line.

"You know, Greg, if you would promise not to do these services anymore, the person bringing the charge would probably drop it."

Dell responded without hesitation, his clear, confident voice full of passion.

"My personal integrity demands that I refuse to make such a promise. I have been appointed to Broadway United Methodist Church to minister to all of the people there," he said, "and since my congregation is 30 percent gay, lesbian or transgendered, retreating from performing union services would be unconscionable. These services have been an important way of responding to the pastoral needs of my parishioners.

"Karl Reinhardt and Keith Eccarius approached me approximately one year before their union service. They did so understanding that I would proceed with them the same way I do with all couples with whom I work. This includes requesting that, if at all possible, we begin meeting at least nine months prior to the service.

"We had completed eight months of counseling when the Judicial Council handed down their ruling. I asked Karl and Keith what they wished to do. They wanted to go ahead, and I felt that I could not retreat from my earlier promise to them and maintain any integrity as their pastor."

Dell paused as if to garner strength. Taking a deep breath, he continued.

"It's unfair to the thousands of people on all sides of this controversial issue to continue debating it in the abstract. The love that God offers is not theoretical. The church must decide if it truly wants to declare that its affirmation of God's embracing, celebrating acceptance is available to some but not to others who want to live in faithful relationships of commitment and love."

Having finished his statement, Dell casually raised his arms and folded his hands behind his head. Fisher noticed the large sweat stains beneath his arms and realized how much raw courage his unwavering stance required.

Hearing Dell's answer, the bishop had no recourse. Concluding that all possibilities for resolution had been exhausted, Sprague outlined the disciplinary process that must be followed, his shoulders sagging with sadness. He adjourned the meeting with a compassionate, earnest prayer.

Sprague hoped that the trial would be a "teachable moment" for the church, showing it and the world "the box we have put ourselves into in this denomination."

1975
naperville · illinois

I had been in a box of my own. As a young mother and housewife, I had first found relief from my suburban restlessness by creating the day care center at our church, Wesley United Methodist, which was named after the founder of the denomination and housed in an English Tudor-style building in downtown Naperville. Subsequently a church study group began to provide some intellectual and social stimulation. After worshipping together as a family, Gary and I took our children to their classes, then joined other adults for the study group.

The group was comprised of 30- to 60-year-old well-groomed and fine-mannered suburbanites who were married with children. The men in our group included several male PhD pastors serving in appointments beyond the local church, a husband/wife team of real estate agents, a medical doctor, a civil engineer and a regional plant manager. The women had completed university bachelor degrees in various fields, worked for a brief time and chosen to become homemakers. Exceptions were one real estate agent, a nurse and a woman working on a master's degree in psychology.

We met in a wood-paneled room in the church basement, which was lit by fluorescent bulbs. The few pieces of brown leather furniture were supplemented by metal folding chairs.

Gathered in a circle for our meetings, we explored how theology and faith intersect in the choices we make daily about our lives. Studies about the greenhouse effect increased my efforts to recycle and encouraged me to notice how political candidates felt about the issue. A unit about the changing role of women confronted me with the fact that, after my children became adults, I would probably have 30 more years to live, much longer than the projected life span of my husband. I found myself considering whether the exclusive role of homemaker would remain satisfying.

One Sunday morning I came to class hoping to be distracted from my growing uneasiness at home. I expected once more to be caught up in a world bigger than my own with people I admired. The agenda wasn't the usual model—a presentation followed by discussion—but I was interested nonetheless.

As soon as we all had greeted one another and had settled in our chairs, Chuck Ellzey, a seminary professor and codirector of our denomination's only research agency, furnished each one of us with a blank piece of paper and a sharpened pencil.

"We're going to do an exercise today that will tell us a lot about one another and ourselves," he said. "If you'll go along with me, I'd like to get started."

We all nodded our assent.

"Good. Then, I want you to write down the name of every person in this room," Chuck said. "Use one line for each name."

We dutifully followed his instruction. When we all looked up, he continued.

"OK. The next part is going to require your imagination. So just relax—this isn't a test. Take a moment to get comfortable in your chair." Waiting patiently for us to stretch our legs and wiggle our bodies into our comfort zones, he continued.

"I want you to make-believe that we're all stranded together on a small island in the Pacific Ocean. There's no one else there but us. Our children, dogs and cats aren't with us—just this group. There might be some wild animals on the island; that isn't clear. And, of course, there are a lot of fish in the ocean surrounding us. We've all arrived well and healthy, but we have no provisions and no shelter. We have no way to communicate with the outside world. OK—got it?"

We looked at one another, smiling in amusement. Elaine shrugged her shoulders, some of us nodded our heads and a few people replied, "Yeah. OK."

"Good. Now I want you to go down your list of people and think about how each one could best contribute to helping our community survive and flourish. You can't talk during this time. I know that some of you might want to ask one another some questions, but that isn't permitted. You might have to do some guessing. After you've thought it through, write beside each name one particular role you think each person could perform for the group to keep us going. Write something you think is vital to our community. Does everyone understand?"

"You mean something like cook or hunter?" asked Andy, an engineer.

"Right," Chuck replied. "And you might need more than one cook or one hunter or something else. That's for you to decide. But try to have all the bases covered when you're through so that every vital role will be done by someone. And be sure to write down a role for yourself as well. I'm going to give you 25 minutes. Since there are 12 of us present this morning, you'll have about two minutes to think about each name. OK? Let's go."

The room became quiet as everyone looked at their paper and thought about the assignment. I closed my eyes and pictured the deserted island beach. Having grown up in Florida, beaches have always been important to me. Suddenly I had a flashback of water skiing for the first time in a cove off Clearwater and remembered how free it had felt to glide over the top of the wet surface with the warm saltwater splashing my face.

In a moment I heard the sound of pencils scratching down answers and realized I needed to focus on the assignment. It was fairly easy to assign roles to everyone else, but I felt puzzled about what to put down for myself. I finally dashed off a neutral answer. Just then, Chuck called us back to order.

"Now, we're going to share what we've written with one another, and this is how we'll do it. We'll start with Gary. Gary will share only what he thinks he could do for us. After he's shared his own idea about his role, I'll go around the room and ask each one of you to share what role you wrote down for him. We'll see how they match up and talk about our results. Then we'll go on to Susan on his right and do the same, continuing around the circle until we're finished. Does everyone understand?"

"Oh, boy, this ought to be good," Jane said nervously. Everyone joined her in laughter. Chuck urged Gary to begin.

"Well, I'm pretty good with tools," Gary said without hesitation. "I realize we'll have to make our own, but I think I could do that, using a rock for a hammer, some palm tree bark strips as rope and some palm leaves for a roof. So I put down that I would build our shelters. I've even got a design in mind."

This surprised no one as the group knew of Gary's training as an architect. The whole class assigned him the same job with the exception of Lois.

"Well, I think you're a pretty good musician, Gary, and I think you might keep us entertained," she said. "So that's what I put down for you: entertainer."

Gary laughed and replied, "But I don't sing a note, and I assume that there won't be a piano or an organ sitting on the beach. So I guess I'd better stick with building our shelter."

"OK, that makes sense," Chuck said. "Let's move on."

Susan shared that she could practice her nursing skills. Once again, everyone agreed. The next few people garnered several role assignments but, as we discussed them, we reached consensus about one job each person could do best. And so it went until, finally, all eyes turned to me.

"Well, I've taught in elementary schools," I started, "but since there will be no children on the island, I can't do that. But I can cook. So I wrote down that I'd be chief cook and bottle washer. I'll join Judy, since she's already been chosen for that role."

"OK," Chuck said. "What did the rest of you put down for Ermalou's role?"

Joe began. "Well, I heard you speak on Laity Sunday, and I thought you did a pretty good job, Ermalou. In fact, I'd like to hear you again. So I think you should be our pastor."

"That's what I put, too," Ellen cried, out of turn.

"Me too," Susan said enthusiastically. Others concurred.

"I wrote down spiritual leader," Chuck said. I also heard your laity address and I've listened to your remarks during our discussions. You've almost always given me a lot to think about." Turning to the others he said, "So does the group agree that Ermalou will be our spiritual leader?" he asked.

"Yes."

"You bet!"

"I'm for it," people responded, smiling at me.

I sat stunned, feeling both thrilled and honored. Then, suddenly, fear flooded me. I entered into one of those moments when pain and joy seem indistinguishable. My hands shook in reaction to what felt like an emotional bomb being thrown my way. With an explosion of elation mixed with terror, I felt at a loss as to what to do.

This group of people I so admired and respected had

inadvertently cracked open my protective shell, exposing a remote and scary place within me that I had occasionally thought about but never really explored (that "other side of the moon"). Even more frightening, they had validated a choice I was afraid of making. I felt grateful for their challenge and respect but was terrified of the demand it placed upon me.

This incident caused me to recall another that had happened when I was 13 years old. I had felt quite uncomfortable one Sunday morning when the Rev. Dr. Lorenzo Dow Patterson stopped me on the sidewalk that ran between First Methodist Church and busy Florida Avenue in downtown Tampa. Patterson was the respected and accomplished associate pastor where my family worshipped.

He looked at me with an intensity that demanded my full attention. In spite of my reluctance, he held my eyes with his. I heard cars whizzing past on the busy street on one side of us and smelled the freshly mown grass of the strip of church lawn on the other side. We were alone in a very public place. He stared at me for what felt like an hour but had to be only a few moments, then proclaimed with certitude, "You're going to become a missionary!"

There was nothing else. No explanation as to why he had come to that conclusion, no reassurance that I could do it, just a strange and powerful proclamation. It rattled me to say the least. I had seen little more of the world than where the slow-moving, fume-belching, passenger-jostling 15th Street bus took me. *How can he think I'd have something to offer people in another country?* I wondered. Geography was my worst subject at school, and I'd never even visited another country.

I walked away from him as quickly as I could, anxious to escape the Florida heat that was intensified by the heat of his proclamation. But his words were seared upon my mind. Too shy to engage him with my questions, I stored this experience away and soon forgot it.

Now the confluence of his pronouncement and the adult study group's confidence in me as a spiritual leader helped me realize I was experiencing what the church terms a "call to ordained ministry." Like other United Methodists, I had been taught that it's the church (non-ordained and clergy alike) that recognizes gifts for pastoral ministry in someone, often long before the person recognizes them in her- or himself.

I felt a spiritual door—deep within me like a root cellar door—being flung open and held there by a strong wind. Today I recognize that wind as Ruach—the breath of God. I felt summoned to go up through the door and see what was on the other side.

Like Robin in *The White Goose*, I hesitated—nervous about choosing between the familiar and Spirit's invitation. I could almost hear the thundering wings of wild geese in flight—a sound that excited me. Yet insecurity caused me to savor this excitement privately for a while. I told Gary nothing about what I was thinking and feeling, and he made no comment about the spiritual gifts the class identified in me.

Later one fall morning, after sending the children to school, I felt compelled to reflect on my life. I sat on the floor in the middle of my living room. A little anxious, I found the carpet's firm support reassuring. The neighborhood was quiet. It was too early for the sounds of lawnmowers. Sunlight streamed through the nearby picture window, calming me. I closed my eyes, relaxed and waited for whatever thoughts would emerge.

What followed became a powerful if strange experience, as I participated in what seemed like a running conversation between two competing forces: my psyche and the Holy One. Questions emerged about what I was doing with my life—questions I hadn't even been aware I was considering. I struggled to answer, then an internal response to my answer would come. It went something like this:

God, I've been thinking ... feeling, really, that I'm supposed to go to seminary. I'm afraid to think about it much. I'm pretty sure that Gary wouldn't like the idea.

So?

Well, what if he's not willing to support me doing this? What if my answering this call causes a divorce?

Answering my call won't cause a divorce. If it happens anyway, I will be with you—always.

But what about our children? What will this do to them?

I will be with them just as I'll be with you. Trust me.

I do trust you, Holy One, but I sure don't trust myself or this situation. In fact, I'm not sure I can even hack it at seminary. I haven't been a student now for 15 years ... and never a graduate student.

You must trust that I will provide. Be not afraid.

And so it went. God affirmed and challenged me—affirming me in having gifts that would be useful to the larger world and challenging me to move beyond my conventional life in order to use them. I became unaware of time passing until, with a start, I heard the front door slam and realized my youngest had come home from school. I had been sitting on the floor for seven hours.

During that time I had nervously decided to explore the process of attending a seminary. I accepted—even embraced—the idea of serving the church full-time, but I still rejected the possibility of becoming a pastor. The idea of such a goal seemed presumptuous, inappropriate and unattainable. Yet I decided to pursue theological studies anyway. *God will show the way*, I thought, and left the outcome to be decided.

When I made inquiries about entering the well-known United Methodist seminary in the area, I discovered I could take a few courses, commuting a total of three hours during the day, and still be home when the children arrived after school.

I felt nervous about Gary's response to this idea because of the dismissive way he had reacted when I first told him about my mystical conversation. I wanted him to support this move emotionally and financially. He only listened quietly.

It wasn't what he said, but the fact that he said so little that put me on edge. I knew that my returning to school would cause a financial strain for us and surmised that this was the reason for his lack of response.

I finally got up my nerve to approach him again one evening after putting the children to bed. He was sitting on our living room couch reading an architectural journal. He responded pleasantly when I asked for his attention, putting down his magazine. I sat down on a chair across the room from him, aware that the heavy glass-topped coffee table separating us offered some psychological protection. I took a deep breath and began.

"Gary, remember the conversation with God I told you about a while back?"

"Yeah, I remember all right. I'm not sure it was God talking to you though," he said with a chuckle. "You have to admit that was weird."

I continued with a serious tone. "Yeah, I agree," I admitted. "I've decided to follow through about it though. In fact, I'm exploring how to get started at Garrett–Evangelical. Now I need to talk with you about how we're going to manage the costs."

I hesitated a moment to see if he had any immediate reaction. When he didn't, I continued. "I might be able to get a scholarship. I think the church back in Tampa has one for seminary students. But it might not be enough. Do you think we can cover the rest?"

He uncrossed his legs, sat forward on the couch, and put his right hand on his knee. His mood changed from mild interest to intense engagement. I felt my body tensing.

"Ermalou, this has been a real surprise. The more I think about it, the more I wonder why you would want to go to seminary. Pastors don't get paid squat! Why don't you shoot for a good career that would pay some money?"

His voice sounded strident, but there was no turning back now. "This isn't about how much money I can earn, Gary. It's about a call. It's about accepting what I believe God wants me to do."

He remained silent for a moment except for a grunt. Finally he spoke again. "When are you thinking of doing this?" he asked quietly.

"Right away, as soon as possible," I replied, aware of but not wanting to acknowledge his discouraging tone.

Suddenly he upped the ante with anger. Throwing his hands into the air he declared, "That's impossible, Ermalou! You aren't thinking straight. You need to put this off until our children are grown. They have to come first with us, right?"

Now my voice took on an edge fueled by my anger. "Good grief, Gary. Assuming you mean when our youngest would be 21, I'd have to wait 14 more years to get started. Is that what you mean?"

"Yes, that should be obvious," he declared.

"I can't believe this," I said. "I put you through school for your second degree. Now it's your turn to do the same for me! My hopes and dreams are just as important as yours are."

"Well, if you're figuring I'm going to live in a crummy parsonage for the rest of my life, forget it! If you go to seminary, you'll have to do it by yourself."

That statement sounded threatening enough to stop me. He picked up his magazine again while I withdrew to the bedroom. I closed the door and thought about our conversation, trying to sort out my pain and confusion. I understood his complaint about parsonages, since his architectural training made our residence an important symbol to him. But his negativity and lack of compassion shocked me. I had not chosen his profession for him. Why did he feel he could and should choose mine? Didn't love mean that you wanted the best for the person you loved? Didn't he love me as much as I had come to love him? It was blatantly apparent that he refused to consider our marriage an equal partnership. I could no longer hide in denial—a realization followed by wrenching sobs that came from deep within me.

When I calmed down, I realized that Gary's need for control was affecting both of us. I once had watched him hold our family cat while he was standing in our yard. He clutched its squirming body tightly so its feet wouldn't touch the ground. When he saw my puzzled expression, he said, "It's strictly an inside cat!" At the time I felt sad—he seemed so afraid to let the cat have the freedom to explore and enjoy the world and find its destiny. Now it dawned on me that he was just as afraid for me to do the same.

However, I decided I would not be denied justice and a level playing field. I determined to continue my investigative efforts whether or not he approved. Soon, in spite of my internal ambivalence about ordained ministry, I went before the committee in my local church that's charged with examining pastoral candidates—just in case I should change my mind. To his credit, Gary wrote a letter to the committee affirming me. I figured this meant he was getting used to the idea and coming around to supporting it.

The Pastor–Parish Relations Committee (PPRC), the church body charged with responsibility for good communication between the congregation and the pastor, listened to my mystical experience and the story of the class's vote and affirmed God's call on my life. None of them revealed personal familiarity with mystical experiences, but they accepted mine based on the many such encounters reported in the Bible.

However, Gary's financial support for seminary still didn't materialize. Undeterred, I contacted Garrett–Evangelical

Theological Seminary in Evanston, Illinois, requesting acceptance into their Masters of Divinity program. Bob Mann, my boss and friend from university days, wrote a letter of endorsement, and I gathered transcripts, the recommendation letter of the PPRC and other required documents. I submitted my complete application and nervously awaited a response.

I didn't wait long. When I spotted a small envelope with the seminary's return address in my mailbox, I quickly took it in with the rest of the mail. I handled it carefully as the life-changing document it promised to be. Alone at the time, I put the other mail on the kitchen table and took the letter to the living room where my conversation with God had taken place.

This time I sat on the couch, my body bent over in a near fetal position and my eyes closed, alert to what felt like a holy and profound moment—a time when what I had heard from God would either be confirmed, encouraging me to go forward, or rejected, dashing my hopes and plans. It took a few moments to gather the courage to open the envelope.

When I did, I read two brief sentences. One congratulated me, and the other invited me to matriculate at the seminary. I held the letter close to my chest and sobbed. After a few moments, I got up and went to the dictionary to look up the meaning of the word "matriculate." The journey to a new world had finally begun.

CHAPTER FOUR

Bishop Joe Sprague secured Bishop Jack M. Tuell to officiate in what would seem much like a civil court proceeding. Tuell, who lived in the Seattle area, had retired after many years of distinguished service as pastor of various churches and as bishop of several conferences. Tall, graying and slightly overweight, he looked like someone's kind grandfather. But his deep and commanding voice, his training as an attorney and his long experience with church matters would serve him well in presiding over the trial.

The 13-member jury of Dell's peers was selected from a pool of Northern Illinois Conference pastors who had not expressed a public opinion on the subject. As in a civil trial, both prosecuting and defense counsels had the opportunity to reject some jury candidates.

Dell selected as his defense counsel the Rev. Dr. Larry Pickens, pastor of Maple Park United Methodist Church in Chicago. Like Bishop Tuell, he was an attorney and ordained clergy. A tall, handsome black man, Pickens' easy, personable style and hint of a Southern drawl often belied his sharp intelligence, giving him the advantage of surprise.

Pickens agreed to act as defense counsel with one caveat: Dell would have to forgo his signature casual attire (a way of identifying with his parishioners) and buy a good suit. When Dell conceded, his wife Jade and Pickens took him shopping.

Bishop Sprague, in accordance with church law, needed to

assign a pastor as church counsel (prosecutor), but finding one had been difficult. After a dozen or so pastors turned down the bishop's request to serve in the position, he expressed his frustration to those who were so adamant about charging Dell and told them to find a prosecutor. At their suggestion, the Rev. Stephen C. Williams was chosen.

Pastor of First United Methodist Church in Franklin Park, Illinois, Williams had transferred 12 years earlier from Pennsylvania to the Northern Illinois Conference with his wife, the Rev. Jamie Hanna Williams.

Most pastors in the conference understood it would be a daunting challenge to serve as either prosecutor or defense. It was difficult for the prosecutor because pastors were trained to give spiritual direction and care, not judgment or punishment. And it was daunting for the defense because Dell had already admitted to breaking church law. The defense's best hope was for the Judicial Council's ruling to be judged invalid. Maybe the court would recognize that Dell's ministry had been faithful and, deeming the new law unfaithful to God's purposes for the church, would permit if not affirm his actions.

The Rev. Fred H. Conger, senior pastor of the host church for the trial, had offered First UMC in Downers Grove as the site due to the persuasion of his associate pastor, the Rev. Dawn Chesser. At first, he naively thought the trial would be a quiet and dignified event. When he realized that political demonstrations were being planned by both sides and that nationwide appeals were being made for people to come to the site to demonstrate their support, he took steps to make the location as neutral as possible to ensure a fair trial

Fearing violence because of the hate crimes that had already occurred nationally around this emotionally charged issue, Conger secured a booklet from the U.S. Bureau of Alcohol, Tobacco and Firearms and Explosives (ATF). The booklet, "BOMB and Physical Security Planning," was designed to prepare for the threat of explosives-related violence. ATF offered to provide a consultant if needed.

In addition to assisting with the bomb scan of the building, the local and county police also worked closely with Conger and agreed to have their best officers on site during the proceedings and to be on alert to rush others there upon his request. A bus with bulletproof windows would be parked unobtrusively around a corner, ready to transport individuals to jail if needed. Every major network asked and was granted permission to park their media trucks on site, as there wouldn't be adequate room for them on Maple Street in front of the church.

Conger and Chesser prepared the members of the local church by keeping them informed about all of the developments. They held classes preceding the trial, featuring speakers from both sides of the issue. On one weekday evening Dell represented his own position as the defendant. On another weekday evening the Rev. Scott Field, pastor of Wheatland Salem UMC in Naperville, who instigated the charges against Dell, explained why he had done so.

Still worried that the trial could turn into a media event with disruptive demonstrations, Conger issued a statement to the press declaring that access to the sanctuary, which would serve as the courtroom during trial proceedings, would be limited. Only trial participants, security people, credentialed news media and members of the public holding tickets for admission would be allowed inside.

Different tickets were printed for each day of the trial and distributed to the trial participants, security, news media and a few church members. The remaining tickets could be secured only from church counsel or defense counsel or through a lottery process conducted by the conference (another irony since the conference opposes gambling). In all, about 400 tickets per day were issued for use in the sanctuary, which holds 450 people.

Media were assigned space in the gym in the lower level of the building to set up their equipment and two adjoining rooms in which to conduct interviews. The entire north parking lot held their media vehicles, and they were granted access to the north door to the building. All other doors, with the exception of the guarded front door, were kept locked throughout the trial. No cameras, video cameras, tape recorders or cell phones, and no bags or briefcases (except those of the presiding bishop and counsel) were allowed in the sanctuary. Press conferences were held outside in the church parking lot.

Conger met with local police every day to discuss developments, and every morning, at his request, officers and their dogs swept the building for bombs. A hundred members of the church were recruited to serve as security guards and were stationed at all doors and throughout the building to enforce the attendance restrictions.

Ruth and Jerry Moyar, a couple in their 60s, were two of those recruited for this job. Their assignment was to sit in an out-of-the-way location guarding a hallway and a door leading to the outside. Both are bright, well educated, active and accomplished people who would have been able to present an excellent argument as to why someone shouldn't be in the hallway. But it would be hard to imagine either of them using force to stop anyone. To do so would probably be beyond their physical strength, to say nothing of their ethical inclinations.

"We had the privilege of going to the sanctuary during our off-duty time, and when we did get to the trial, Jerry and I always sat in the balcony," Ruth said. "The mood in the church was tense and excited. Everyone seemed on edge. Once I saw an usher—someone I know to be conservative—turn on his heels and declare, 'This is an abomination!' But I think most of the people there hoped, like us, that Greg would be acquitted."

I traveled to the seminary for the first time on a wintry day. The 90-minute drive from Naperville to Evanston felt tense as I shifted my eyes back and forth from my map to the road, slowing carefully at times so the car didn't slide on the ice. The January air felt crisp and cold. I hadn't yet become accustomed to driving far distances in winter. At every red traffic light I stewed about being late. But finally I arrived at the glorious old Gothic building with its tall, church-like steeple.

I am officially a student at Garrett–Evangelical Theological Seminary, I thought, smiling. I reveled in the sheer accomplishment of this moment, knowing it would soon be forgotten as new challenges presented themselves.

The eight-foot-high wood doors seemed to offer one last resistance to my quest. I pushed them open with determination and found my way upstairs to Room 205, where Dr. Paul Hessert, Professor of Systematic Theology, would expose me to the academic world of the seminary. Among other things, this involved learning a language foreign to me, including words like "eschatology" and "hermeneutics." He and other professors would also present the ancient world to me in a fresh way so I might help reshape the world around me, looking through the lens of Jesus. All this lay ahead of me.

Meanwhile, I sat smelling a familiar musty classroom odor. Although not the only woman in the class, at 36 I was the oldest. Sitting in a student's chair made me feel like a kid again, as insecure as I had been when I started grammar school and with just as much nervous first-day excitement.

The bell rang for the class to begin while a few students hurried to their seats. I felt surprised at their appearance: T-shirts over rumpled jeans; long, shaggy hair on the men; simple drip-dry hairstyles on the women; dirty sneakers or scuffed shoes on many feet. I realized my navy blue pants suit, dress shoes, styled hair and carefully applied makeup made me a little too put together to fit in. I nervously checked once more to make sure my ballpoint pen had ink.

Dr. Hessert entered with his arms full of papers, which he dumped on the lectern at the front of the room. A small man, he had a serious face and earnest eyes. His smile looked perfunctory, as if it had been pinched into place like the mouths of the Play-Doh characters my children fashioned. He had dressed casually—no suit or tie, just nice trousers and a dress shirt under a pullover sweater. He walked with a slight limp and seemed as nervous as the rest of us.

"Hello," he said, his voice sounding boyish and embarrassed, "and welcome to The History of Theology I." After another forced smile, he began passing out a sheet of paper to each student from one of the stacks on the lectern.

"Here is my list of required reading for the class," he said. "The books that have an asterisk in front of them are available in the bookstore. The rest you can find in the library. You'll need to read and write a report on at least two books from each area."

The list seemed formidable, a whole page of single-spaced, typed entries of theological tomes divided into three categories. As soon as he finished passing out the sheets, he began his lecture. Now his voice became full of authority. He began moving about easily, illustrating his lecture points with quickly sketched line drawings, names, dates and charts on the chalkboard behind him. I sat impressed and transfixed through it all, feeling the joy of being intellectually challenged again, yet a bit overwhelmed at all I would need to learn just to keep up.

Back at home, Gary seemed to be tolerating my decision but offered no emotional support. I reached out to two new friends who I thought would provide encouragement. Chuck and his wife, Marge, were both members of the Sunday morning adult class; Chuck had led the group exercise that resulted in my being chosen as the group's spiritual leader. I continued to be nourished by the class, thrilled that for the first time in my life I could be part of a group of people who actually struggled out loud about how to make faith part of all life, including politics, relationships, government, finances, child rearing, work and world view. Yet I wanted more.

Soon I drew together four couples, including Chuck and Marge, into a small group that served as a class extension. We met one evening a month in each other's homes. Our discussions were rich and interesting, which satisfied that motive for forming the group. I also secretly hoped that being around Chuck more in a group setting would defuse the strong attraction I had developed for him. The opposite happened. Confused and bewildered, I kept my feelings to myself.

I turned my attention to music, which became a cathartic force allowing me to express my jumble of emotions. I composed eight songs, added dialogue to tie them together and presented a musical at the church as a benefit. I named the program, "It Feels Good" after the final song, which expresses the joy of a women feeling liberated from the emotional/spiritual bindings of cultural expectations. The music gave voice to the many current responses to women's liberation—including a chauvinistic one—all leading to the final title song.

About 20 church friends agreed to participate as dancers, musicians, speakers and stagehands. One friend, Linda White, scored the songs for me. Chuck and Marge, both members of the choir, agreed to join the cast, enriching the production and adding to the great fun we all had together. Marge asked to revise a couple of lines of the lyrics they would be performing in order to give them deeper meaning. I accepted her suggestions gratefully, resulting in the final lyrics:

You've gotta take a chance at living the educated, liberated
life!
You'll never know in advance who'll end up wearing the
pants
 but you won't care, 'cause you can share everything.
The joy of rearing all the little children, the happiness of
corporation strife;
They may be equal parts of living the educated, liberated
life.

You've gotta take a chance while living the educated,
liberated life.
I'll share my paycheck with you; we'll be much richer with
two.
 and that's fair, 'cause we can share everything.
The chores that were traditionally divided between the
average man and his wife,
We'll both take equal parts of bearing in the educated,
liberated life.

It's worth the chance you take of living an educated,
liberated life!
You'll find it's better by far to be the person you are
without regret;
 one that will bet everything,
On the growth that comes from feeling every feeling,
And knowing joy and fear and love and strife,
Are valid parts of what's called living the educated,
liberated life!

"You've Gotta Take a Chance." Ermalou M. Roller, 1975.

Marge and Chuck did a wonderful job singing their duet,
and through the practices, I got to know them better.
An attractive woman with dancing eyes, Marge laughed easily,

spreading her contagious enthusiasm. We chuckled that she could get to know a stranger standing in line better than we knew some of our relatives.

She attended a nearby college, where she worked on an advanced degree. Although she didn't feel too keen about the institutional church, we shared an interest in feminism. After hearing her ideas in the adult class, I encouraged her to expand on them by creating a course for women at the church. She did so, engaging participants to prepare for the long life most women will have after children have left the nest.

Chuck's hazel-green eyes were the kindest I'd ever seen, and they often sparkled with laughter. Slim, articulate and engaging, he had grown long, wide sideburns, as many men did in the '70s. His full head of brown hair had one gray streak on the right side at the back of his head.

I admired his relaxed confidence, his understanding of and love for the church, and the interesting way he brought together what I would later learn are classic theological disciplines and applied behavioral sciences. He never seemed defensive about his positions and patiently encouraged others to clarify their own thoughts. So it felt safe to risk expressing and exploring ideas with him, even ideas that challenged his own.

Playfulness and a willingness to quietly confront oppression added to his already impressive attributes. I remember one morning in the class when his chair sat next to mine on my right. I felt a bit uncomfortable about our proximity and scooted my chair a bit to the left. He immediately scooted his chair left as well and, when I looked up in surprise, he gave me a charming grin.

Another time, he listened to Gary rant on to the class about what some woman had done and how "if Ermalou ever did that I would divorce her!" Gary emitted a loud, phony laugh after this pronouncement as he often did when he didn't feel sure how a comment would be received. No one joined in the fake revelry.

The class became quiet for a moment, embarrassed with and for me. Chuck, his face calm but determined, said, "Well, you know, don't you, Gary, that Ermalou could also divorce you?"

"Oh I guess anything's possible," Gary replied with another phony laugh.

Chuck served as codirector of our denomination's only research agency, the Center for Parish Development. He had also taught as a fully tenured professor at Garrett–Evangelical Theological Seminary and had served the UMC as a pastor. An impossible ham, he took every opportunity to crack a corny joke, sing a song or expertly perform some knife-throwing trick learned in his growing-up years at his family's cattle ranch in Texas.

He dressed in conservative suits with atrociously loud shirts and ties. I remember one in particular: a neon orange shirt topped off with a green-and-yellow-striped tie. I think the sideburns and the bright-colored clothing were his attempt at being "hip" and "with it." I could tell he liked being a bit of a rebel.

Gary, who valued smart clothing, would look at him and shake his head in disdain over Chuck's cavalier dismissal of fashion. I usually stifled a giggle and rolled my eyes about the whole thing. I felt so enchanted with Chuck's mind and spirit I couldn't have cared less about how he dressed. In fact, I found it endearing.

When I received my acceptance letter from the seminary, I decided to tell Marge and Chuck. I had, of course, already told Gary, but he had seemed most interested to hear that I had also been awarded a scholarship from the United Methodist Women. However, I felt certain that Chuck and Marge would share my excitement and provide some much needed support. I called their home one morning with the intention of making an appointment to meet them both. Marge answered. When I told her I wanted to see them and why, she responded enthusiastically.

"Oh, come on over now. I'm going to be home all day and we can just talk."

"Are you sure?" I said. "I can come tonight or some other time."

"No, you can tell Chuck later. Come on over. I'll make tea."

"Well, the children are in school right now," I said. "I'll be there shortly."

She smiled as she met me at the door, dressed casually in slacks and a blouse. My anticipation of her spirit of acceptance and celebration proved to be correct. She invited me to sit down in their living room, served me hot tea, slipped out of her shoes and put her feet up on the couch. She listened to my story with appreciation, and we talked about my decision for a while. Suddenly she grabbed the steering wheel of our conversation and gave it a startling turn.

The topic of conversation? Marge's sexual needs and how she was dealing with them. She talked with admiration about a woman close to her, a radical feminist engaged in a lesbian relationship. Then, after a break to refill our teacups, she revealed that she and Chuck had recently decided to test a new approach to their own relationship by experimenting in open marriage.

I worked hard to keep up, honored that she trusted me enough to share so intimately, but becoming increasingly confused by her ideas. I interrupted her. "What does that mean, an open marriage?"

"Well, Chuck went to a seminar with me a few weeks ago here in town. One of my professors recommended the seminar for extra credit. And it was really good."

"Did it deal with the open marriage thing?" I said impatiently.

"Oh, no," she replied, her eyes dancing with excitement. "It dealt with healthy sexual development."

"Oh. OK."

"And afterward, Chuck and I had a long talk about the fact that we had married without having any sexual experience with others. And that maybe, you know, that hadn't been a good idea."

She paused in contemplation, crossing her bare feet underneath her on the couch and sipping more tea before continuing.

"Chuck and I never seem to be at the same place at the same time emotionally, you know?"

I didn't but wanted her to continue, so I nodded my head.

"We almost didn't marry. We went together for a long time in college and got engaged, then I broke it off. I told him I felt unsure. The truth was, he wasn't the kind of guy who turned me on."

"Really?" I asked, surprised.

"Yeah," she responded, once more brightening. "I liked the football types better!" she said, laughing. "But after a while, I came back to Chuck. He had waited for me and so we got married."

"Well, what's this open marriage stuff about?" I asked, trying to conceal growing excitement.

"Oh, right. Well, after the seminar, we decided to give one another the freedom to have sexual experiences with others if we decide that we want to. I mean, if we feel drawn to that with someone. We don't want a divorce or anything. It's just a growth thing. We think it will be good for both of us."

"Wow," I replied, awed and shocked but trying to appear nonchalant. "Has either of you acted on it yet?"

"Well, Chuck has. A woman came to the seminar and, at the end, wanted to see him. They had been in the same small group there, and he's responded to her. I don't think it's just about the sex. I don't think that's what's really important to either of them. She has some sexual problems; that's why she came in the first place. So I think it's just about hugging."

Then, laughing again, she added, "You know how much Chuck likes to hug people!"

"Yeah, he challenges guys to hug each other too," I said, "and they're obviously uncomfortable about that. He seems to enjoy making them squirm!"

"He does," she responded, smiling. Returning to his new

relationship, she continued, "I've called this woman and we've had friendly discussions on the phone—several of them, in fact. And I'm not worried that she's any kind of threat or anything, you know, to our marriage."

"Well, that's good," I responded, amazed that she seemed so comfortable with this arrangement, so friendly with the other woman and so sure about their marriage. But then she wondered out loud what would happen if Chuck ever left her. "Who would put the storm windows up," she asked, "or mow the grass?"

My mind reeled at the pothole-filled road she had chosen to take us on, moving from listening to my story to pouring out her soul and revealing intimate details about her sexuality and her marriage.

I listened with one part of my mind. With the other part, I thought about reports in recent news magazines of the cultural phenomenon sweeping the country. Many disillusioned couples were trying a variety of things to make their marriages fresh again. A best-selling book entitled *Open Marriage: A New Life Style for Couples*, by Nena and George O'Neill, reported the most radical of these efforts. The authors claimed to have agreed that each of them could have casual sexual encounters with others.

Flouting long-held values and Puritan-inspired attitudes, this book caught and held media attention. The O'Neills' approach, only one of a continuum of experiments going on, included challenging sexual boundaries. The common factor in all of them was the desire of people to find a way to openly and ethically address the void in their lives so they could live more fully while remaining in a valued marriage.

My mind returned to the room, which suddenly seemed hot. Was it the tea or the conversation? My friend made another sharp jerk of the wheel, abruptly turning the conversation back to me.

"I told Chuck that you think he hung the moon," she said brightly, with a friendly little laugh. Then she added, "I can appreciate that you two might become special friends. You have a lot in common."

I had never heard that expression about the moon but guessed that she meant how much I admired and liked her husband—perhaps even knew I had developed a crush on him. I felt invaded and vulnerable. She had exposed private, forbidden longings I had expected to always remain private. I didn't know how to reply. I had come to share my seminary news with her, but now she was clearly driving this conversation, and it had careened out of my control. Embarrassed, I looked at the floor. When I looked up again, she had a faraway look in her eyes.

"It's strange that two women are in love with my husband, and I've never felt that way about him," she said thoughtfully.

She sat calmly. Was she having fun with me, oblivious to the danger all around us, or was she strangely unafraid? I couldn't tell, but her stillness allowed me to settle down. I breathed in deeply and hoped she didn't hear me as I let out a deep sigh. Then I did it again.

Finally, I followed my second impulse (the first being to run like hell, but my pride, or perhaps unrecognized desperation, wouldn't let me be that much of a coward). *These are really cool people*, I thought, *and I don't want to seem like a prude to them.* My nerve returned. Since she had been so open with me, I decided to come clean with her. The possibility of being involved with Chuck under these safe circumstances seemed enticing.

"Would it be OK with you if I tell Chuck how I feel?" I asked nervously.

She remained quiet for another moment. "Yes, I have no problem with that," she said. "But I'd like to be present when you tell him." Another silence followed.

I heard the unmistakable inner sound of another soul door swinging wide open—a door as full of danger and promise as that root cellar door connected to my call. Or was it the same door? Was this invitation a demonic force competing with my call to ministry or God's provision of abundance to a hungry pilgrim? I felt thoroughly confused but took no more time to ponder the question.

Excited and impressed by her confidence in their relationship, her continued friendliness toward the extra woman and her apparent understanding that I had no intention of harming either of them, I rushed through the inner door, once more leaving familiar, and what had seemed like solid ground behind me. I thanked her for her hospitality and her encouragement and left, knowing that I needed to talk with Gary before doing anything out of the ordinary.

On the way home I drove slowly, excited but agitated about following through with Gary and with Chuck. I hadn't made a close male friend in many years—just acquaintances. I certainly hadn't ever considered expanding the sexual boundaries of my marriage—until now. I couldn't decide if talking with Chuck about my feelings and proposing to spend more time together felt appropriate. But I knew immediately that I wanted to.

Lacking a parental model of marriage to ground me and feeling that cultural norms about marriage were no longer working for me, I decided I needed to make my own way. If my anxiety was the voice of reason urging me to stop, my joy was a sign of the cacophony of intriguing possibilities propelling me forward.

That night, after I tucked the children into their beds, I told Gary about the morning conversation and of my interest, by now solid, in conducting our own experiment in an open marriage. I carefully explained that I would like this to include granting one another sexual freedom, citing how well this was working for Marge and Chuck. Once more I hoped, at best, to dissipate my strong attraction to Chuck or, at least, to learn what this experiment could tell me about myself that I needed to fix.

Appreciating the radical nature of the concept of open marriage, I made as strong a case as I could to him that, whatever happened, it would not be threatening to our relationship. My intentions were impeccable, my resolve clear. I would be faithful to whatever agreement we reached. Given all this, I asked if he would have any objections to my following through with Chuck.

After thinking about it for a few days and enduring my lobbying, Gary reluctantly went along. He felt concerned about what all this would lead to. I reassured him it wouldn't be a problem and could be valuable to my personal development.

As we began to see one another, Chuck gently ended the relationship with the woman he had been seeing, saying that although he was grateful for the way they had helped one another through a time of transition in their lives, they were not suited for a long-term connection.

We began to regularly engage in activities that Gary and my women friends didn't enjoy. We had long philosophical discussions, played tennis on local courts—occasionally waving to mutual friends—and shared our common zest for life. I felt grateful to discover a way to fill out the empty and lonely places of my life. I found him absolutely charming, creative and full of information and experiences I felt eager to explore. Chuck loved to teach (something he no longer did regularly), and I realized that, by respecting and enjoying him as a mentor and a cherished friend, I also filled out empty and lonely places in his life. So although our education and life experiences were different, we bonded easily. He was 51 years old; I was 35.

As our relationship developed, Chuck and I never seemed to have enough time to talk. At first our conversations included childhood stories, theological discussions and shameless bragging to impress one another. I heard about his breathtaking blind landing in a field when his plane suddenly lost power during training as a Navy pilot. He felt so proud that neither the plane nor he had suffered any damage because he had kept his eyes on the lights of a small city beneath him, using them to adjust his landing gear.

He told me about the family ranch in Texas, his wonderful extended clan there and the boy's ranch he had helped run as a youngster. He talked about the unique brand for their cattle (LZ), which he explained is the phonetic version of the family's surname, Ellzey.

He heard about my brief student broadcasting stint as one of the first women staff on air at WTUN, the University of Tampa radio station and about how the *Tampa Tribune* had featured our story and printed pictures of us on "Ladies Day" in 1958. The paper reported that it would be the first time in the history of Tampa radio that a station would operate for an entire day without the aid of a single man anywhere.

I also bragged openly about the achievements and charms of my children, Kathy, Michael and Stan, and shared my ongoing struggle to keep up my exercise routine each day in spite of a jammed schedule. We soon moved beyond all need to impress one another, and our conversations became more real, relaxed and current.

One day we drove to a local forest preserve. We felt pleased to be alone in the parking lot. For a while we sat snugly in the car, holding hands and silently enjoying the freshly fallen snow through the windshield. The empty tree limbs etched in white were breathtakingly beautiful. Fat squirrels and an occasional bird provided the only movement or sound.

Relishing the intimate mood, I confessed a new fear regarding seminary.

"Chuck, there aren't too many other students my age. They're all so young. I feel a little silly having taken so long to figure out what I want to do with my life. It's really embarrassing!" I said, feeling my face heat up.

He listened quietly, running his hand through his hair, and

replied, "I can understand how you feel, precious woman [his favorite name for me], but you don't seem to realize the kind of personal power you have."

"What do you mean by personal power?" I asked, puzzled.

He turned to face me, took both of my hands in his and looked directly at me with his now serious, always kind, hazel-green eyes. "I mean that you are strong, clear, articulate and determined. You have the gift of being able to conceptualize in a discussion and, most of all, you care about people. That shows through all by itself, and people see these things. Maybe you don't understand this now, but trust me, you're going to have a lot of respect and admiration. In fact, I expect you will be a role model, especially for the women students." He stopped, grinned and then continued, "Besides, I think you're beautiful!"

Embarrassed yet pleased by his praise, I blushed, smiled and hugged him, tucking away his compliments so I could relish them again and again whenever I needed reassurance.

Chuck's ongoing attention caused me to remember how I had first enjoyed the pleasure of relaxed, spontaneous affection as a baby only to have it disappear when Dad died and Mother became so tired and sad. I responded by nearly dying with pneumonia. Later, as a young girl, a neighbor offered me the spontaneous affection I had been missing.

Mrs. Rodriguez was a nice neighbor. Tall, large around the middle, with an undefined, rounded bosom, she pulled her dark hair into a bun on the back of her head and wore what Mother called sensible shoes. She spoke broken but understandable English, having fled, along with several of our other neighbors, from Cuba to avoid the Batista regime. We often played with her grandson Pepe.

The Spanish-speaking Rodriguez family ("foreigners" in our midst) lived across the street from us. They always treated us with respect and exposed me to different ways of thinking, behaving and speaking. Some differences were situational; others were cultural.

In addition to having a male head of the household, their home was immaculate, with throw rugs covering the waxed wood floors. Our house—unsupervised while Mom was at work—was always a mess, with bare floors grainy from children's bare feet tracking in the Florida sand. Mrs. Rodriguez stayed at home and often baked goodies; Mom served us fresh fruit for dessert. Like her Hispanic sisters, Mrs. Rodriguez cooked with a lot of garlic, which I had never tasted even though its strong fragrance permeated our neighborhood. Her household consisted of three generations, including grandchildren. Their family was Roman Catholic; we were Protestant.

We bought our bread at the grocery store and noted that a long, skinny loaf of bread was delivered early every morning to the Rodriguez house. Still wrapped in the palmetto leaves in which it was baked, the fresh bread was slapped onto a porch nail where it hung until the family collected it. Everyone in this household, even the young children, ate this bread dunked in strong Cuban coffee for breakfast, which would have been unthinkable for anyone in our family.

However, the biggest difference between our family and theirs was the unembarrassed, open affection their family showed to one another. Children especially were hugged tightly, kissed repeatedly, and their hair tousled by any nearby relative. And the children expressed their pleasure at all of this with loud giggles.

I watched these affectionate exchanges from across the street, wishing our family could be more like theirs. Occasionally Mrs. Rodriguez would catch me watching and smile warmly. Although we never said more than a friendly hello now and then or exchanged a wave of the hand, and although I felt embarrassed when she saw me watching, her friendly smile nurtured my lonely heart.

One lovely summer day, I went outside to play on my red

scooter. By then a six-year-old tomboy, I loved zooming up and down the sidewalk in front of our house. Live oak trees lined each side of the street, their long limbs meeting to form a high arch over the brick street, creating the kind of space professional landscapers like to design. I enjoyed watching the interesting patterns created by the filtered light. A single mockingbird competed with several blue jays to belt out the most authentic song.

As I sped along, I watched carefully for the cracks in the sidewalk. After navigating several fast runs, I noticed that Mrs. Rodriguez had come out of her house on the other side of the street and stood watching me. I allowed my scooter to slow and stuck my foot out to bump to a stop.

"Hello, Mrs. Rodriguez," I called across the street.

She looked a little strangely at me, which made me feel nervous. Had I done something wrong? Was she mad at me?

After a second or two I saw her great toothy smile as she called out in her heavy Spanish accent, "Come over here, you cute little thing, and let me give you a great big kiss!"

Terrified by her invitation, I dropped my scooter, turned and ran as fast as I could toward the safety of my home. But she crossed the street and ran faster. My fear intensified as I heard her heavy footsteps catching up to me. Soon she caught me from behind and gathered me up into her strong arms, laughing loudly and planting sloppy wet kisses all over my face and neck. Her breath was heavy with garlic.

Competing feelings engulfed me: warmth, embarrassment, pleasure and horror. Finally I lived up to my nickname by squirming away, running home and lying on my bunk bed for hours trying to recover from the sick feeling in my stomach. The lingering smell of garlic still enveloped me along with something even more powerful and lasting: the memory of her playful pursuit, loving touch and abundant kisses. Although such open, uninhibited expressions of affection had become foreign to me, they were strangely and deeply satisfying—part of a long-lost, precious memory just out of reach of my consciousness.

My dad's death had created a void of spontaneous affection in my life. Although I still longed for it, warm physical affection had become foreign—even frightening. So much later, when Mrs. Rodriguez' wet kisses reawakened memories of how it had felt, I ran away and emotionally shut down.

When I married, I expected to finally reclaim the joy of spontaneous affection, to feel relaxed and uninhibited about receiving and expressing sensual pleasure, and to fully adore my partner and feel adored by him. But none of this happened, and no matter how hard I worked to make myself more attractive and pleasing to Gary, our intimate times proved to be more mechanical than fulfilling. Once more I coped by shutting down, blaming myself and staying busy with my life of cherished children and meaningful community service.

Now, with Chuck, the long-suppressed torrent of sensual desire came gushing forth like a powerful yet benign force of nature, overwhelming me. The fact that both of our partners agreed to our relationship being sexual freed us from guilt. We felt like kids who had been given the keys to a candy shop—with the admonition not to eat ourselves sick and to come home soon.

Chuck felt surprised and enchanted by my passionate abandon and I by his. Strangely, neither of us felt uncomfortable or shy with one another even though we were testing what was for us radical new behavior. I felt any lingering fear being swept away. In fact, I felt like I had become a whole person and, in some mysterious but important way, a woman for the first time.

The way he held me in his arms felt amazingly different than anything I had experienced with Gary, my only other lover. He touched me so gently for one thing, with a combination of reverence, wonder and grace. He cherished all our moments together and wanted to make them last as long as possible rather than just rushing us toward a crescendo of feeling. And most of all, Chuck enjoyed, even delighted, in every part of my body. Gary's earlier comment to me about women's breasts now seemed ludicrous.

Deliriously happy, I could not give or receive enough to be satiated. I enjoyed the way Chuck thought, the feel of his craggy face beneath my fingers, the way he laughed so easily. I reveled in the way his creative spirit always saw another way of looking at and of doing everything, his kindness and the look in his eyes each time he saw me—everything. Being together felt like rich, deep worship. I often cried hot tears of joy while he held me, and I whispered prayers of thanksgiving to God for the chance of knowing such profound love.

Six months passed, and I became aware that our spouses were hurt. Our friendship hadn't gone as they had expected. No doubt they both noticed the differences in our demeanor. We felt so happy, alive in new ways and impatient to see one another again. Because they had agreed to this experiment and we continued to be open about seeing one another, they lived with their growing pain.

Then, in spite of ourselves, Chuck and I began to look forward to being together more than being with our partners. Although we had pledged to not allow our relationship to threaten our marriages and sincerely meant that promise, it clearly began to do just that.

I found a counselor, and Gary and I began marriage therapy, a process I found to be excruciatingly tedious. But all four of us realized that things had gotten out of hand. Gary demanded that I immediately end my extra relationship, and our marriage therapist promptly backed him up. There were too many voices for me to take on now, voices happy to use the guilt card on me. So I agreed and broke it off with Chuck because I didn't want to lose my husband over this conflict. *Surely, in time*, I thought, *I'll figure a way out of this morass.*

CHAPTER FIVE

T he day of the trial, advocates from both sides of the issue planned rallies near the church. Dell backers, organized into an effective Defense Strategy Team, helped visitors with parking, transportation and housing. Lunch and dinner times found most people congregated at the Pizza Capri on nearby Main Street. The team leased Fishel Park, where about 50 to 60 persons gathered peacefully for a daily vigil at 8:00 AM. Many stayed throughout the day and into the evening in the clear, cold air. The team also provided signs for supporters to carry. They read:

"Justice for some = Injustice for all."

"The love between a gay couple is a God-given blessing."

"God's intention is inclusion."

Phil Stanton and his wife, Delta, who had gay friends, were happy to be there taking a stand. Phil had gone on disability a few years earlier after suffering a stroke that left his right side semi-paralyzed. Yet they decided to drive the more than 700 miles from their home in Binghamton, New York, to Downers Grove for the trial. When asked why he had come, Phil replied, "It was a no-brainer."

"Yes," Delta agreed. "We stayed at the home of the Moyars, who are very nice people. It meant so much to me to be with other supporters, standing together, walking around the park and singing. We were anxious for justice to be served and knowing it was kind of iffy."

A few randomly organized people picketed on the sidewalk

by Maple Street in front of the church carrying hateful signs about "faggots" and "queers," which elevated the fear factor. But Phelps and his 1,000 marchers never materialized.

The trial began at 9:30 AM on the morning of Thursday, March 25, in a closed session. During this time the Trial Court (jury) was selected by the two opposing counsels. By noon the required 13 members and two alternates were seated. Bishop Tuell declared a recess for lunch with the understanding the court would resume at 1:00 PM and the proceedings would then be open for those who had secured admission tickets.

As soon as the front doors of the church were opened, clergy and lay people gathered in the sanctuary. Their business-like clothing seemed to attest to the somber nature of the proceedings—there was not a pair of jeans in the crowd.

Nervous chatter filled the large, long room, reverberating off the dark vaulted ceiling and bouncing back to the red carpet, which promptly muted it. The space looked odd to churchgoers since the chancel furniture had been temporarily removed and replaced by a long wooden table and two chairs, one for use by the presiding bishop and the other for witnesses. At the end of the raised chancel and down several steps onto the main floor, a long bench against the wall, usually used by acolytes on Sunday mornings, was reserved for the counsel to sit side by side.

Although it was nearly Palm/Passion Sunday, no banners or flowers were in the room. Natural light filtering through the yellow and gold glass windows enhanced the illumination provided by the large Gothic fixtures hanging by chains from the ceiling.

At the front of the sanctuary, beyond the bishop's table, was the empty choir loft and above it a large stained-glass rendering of Jesus in rich hues of red, purple, gold and turquoise. The stained-glass Good Shepherd held a lamb in his left arm and a shepherd's staff in his right hand. This illustrated the story Jesus reportedly told of how the good shepherd will leave his whole flock to rescue just one lost sheep. For some present, there was a jarring disconnect between this well-known, well-loved allegory and the beginning of a trial that would decide whether to chastise a pastor for taking this lesson seriously.

Bishop Joe Sprague decided to absent himself from the trial except to testify and listen to the reading of the verdict. He felt it was inappropriate for the resident bishop to be there at other times. Since his views were widely known, he understood that his presence might unfairly influence the jury. He stayed in touch with his superintendents by cell phone and asked that they report to him at every break. Rev. Field, who had made the complaint against Dell, had no such ethical constraints. He made himself highly visible and available to the press at every opportunity.

When all the parties had arrived and the room was full, Bishop Tuell reconvened the trial with his deep, resonate voice. After prayer and introductory remarks, he reminded those gathered that this was not a civil court but one that would be ruled and governed by *The Book of Discipline of the United Methodist Church*.

He explained that the trial would be open according to Dell's wishes and read the formal charge for all to hear:

"In the matter of Rev. Gregory R. Dell, there is one charge and one specification.

"Charge: The Rev. Gregory R. Dell is charged with the offense of disobedience to the order and discipline of the United Methodist Church under paragraph 2624.1e of the 1996 *Book of Discipline*.

"Specification: That on or about September 18, 1998, Rev. Gregory R. Dell conducted a service celebrated as one of holy union between Mr. Keith Eccarius and Mr. Karl Reinhardt, two males."

"And at this time, it's my duty to ask the Respondent, Mr. Dell, would you stand, Mr. Dell, so that I may ask you this question? What is your plea to this charge?"

Dell rose and said, "I plead not guilty, Bishop."

As Dell sat down, Church Counsel Williams stood to make his opening statement. He spoke calmly but passionately.

"As many of you know, I did not seek or desire this assignment. When Bishop Sprague asked me to serve as church counsel several months ago, I asked for 24 hours to think it over. And during that time, I sensed quickly that there was something more at stake than simply processing the Complaint the bishop had signed. I sensed that the honor of our judicial process was at stake. And I felt then and more so now that the honor of our church and the honor of the Order of Elders was bound up in this moment.…"

Williams continued his opening statement by citing the vows and responsibilities of pastors to uphold church law as introduction to Dell's disobedience.

"Rev. Gregory Dell conducted a homosexual union ceremony at Broadway United Methodist Church on September 19, 1998.…

"As we will prove, the Respondent did this knowingly, willfully and without regard for the authoritative binding ruling of the Judicial Council that to conduct such a ceremony is … a disciplinary violation.

"The Respondent did this not because there was any doubt about the law, but rather because he disagreed with the law. He insists that he will go on doing these ceremonies, regardless of the teaching of our church. In short, the Respondent challenges us, as ordained elders, to stand up for our covenant community and to honor our ordination vow set forth in the *Discipline* to hold each other accountable for the sake of the life and mission of the church.…

"This is a grave and solemn moment. And eight and a half million Methodists and all of Christendom wait to see if accountability really counts in the church, which we believe is the salt of the earth and the light of the world....

"We are called here today in defense of the church's right to define its ministry under its law. And a threat to this right is nothing less than a threat to the church's very existence....

"Notwithstanding his personal disagreement with 65C [the new Judicial Council ruling number] and his high regard for the Respondent which he has also made public, it was Bishop Sprague who brought these charges.... [He] recognized you can't just break the law just because you disagree with it. And when it is your responsibility to enforce the law, you can't ignore the law just because you disagree with it.

"Indeed, he will tell you last October his choice was stark. Either to sign the Complaint or resign his office.

"We suggest that the Respondent had the same duty...."

Following his remarks, three witnesses were called to testify for the church: Bishop George Bashore, president of the Council of Bishops; Dell; and Bishop Sprague. They all concurred, due to Williams' sharply honed questions, that Dell had broken church law.

With that, Williams announced that, subject to rebuttal, the church rested its case.

Defense Counsel Pickens stood and made his opening statement, saying that the Trial Court had been given, "an awesome responsibility." This is, he said, "a case about willful ministry ... about the willingness to meet people where they are ... about the human side of ministry."

He continued: "The church counsel would have you believe that this is about the law and the letter of the law and that somehow what Reverend Dell did ... threatens the very existence of the church. I only ask you the question: then are we ever allowed to question?

"In a sense, I would suggest to you that it's really the United

Methodist Church that is on trial tonight because what we have to determine is whether the covenant is a set of rigid, legalistic rules and regulations or whether it is an organic and expansive living community in which our dialogue and faith experiences serve to allow us to live together in a dynamic tension of life and faith.

"This case is about the tension that is already present in our polity.... The restriction that we place on our pastors as it relates to the performance of same sex unions and the requirement that our pastors be in ministry to all persons within a contextual framework serve as a confusing contradiction....

"We are facing theological schizophrenia in our church.... Gregory Dell is a theological and ecclesiastical casualty...."

Pickens cited how John Wesley had pragmatically ordained elders and a bishop during his work in the American colonies, even though the church had not given him the authority to do so. "If John Wesley had followed a rigid adherence to church law, none of us here today would have valid credentials of ordination. We are here today in the spirit of John Wesley....

"We invite you to open your minds, your hearts and your spirits to the dwelling of the Holy Spirit, a spirit that is not bound by strictures of rule but is a spirit that transforms and brings renewal to God's people in all generations....

"This case is about the character and the soul of our church. We will submit our case to you and ask that you would give us a fair hearing and may God help all of us as we lead our church into the next century...."

He proceeded to question the eight witnesses he had arranged for, beginning with an expert on church polity: Dr. Thomas E. Frank, Professor of Religious Leadership and Administration and Director of Methodist Studies at Candler School of Theology. Frank's witness addressed two major points: (1) Historically our preachers have related with one another through a covenant of community, where the tensions within were expected to be dealt with by simply sitting down and talking with one another; (2) The specific meaning of the phrase "order and discipline" is never defined anywhere in the *Discipline*. "Therefore," he said, "it is difficult to charge anyone with disobeying what is not defined."

After Pickens' questioning of the witness, Frank was questioned by Williams. Following this, Pickens engaged in the redirect examination of Frank.

Pickens asked, "Dr. Frank, in your opinion, does violation of a single rule constitute a violation of the covenant or disobedience to the order and discipline of the church?"

Frank: "I don't see how it could. United Methodist clergy violate single rules all the time. So do United Methodist laity.... If you go back to the general rules that govern the life of the first Methodist societies in the 18th century, they were not nearly so much rules about specific acts as they were about the formation of persons, the character of persons. Wesley … tried to show that Methodism was not about legalism.... What Methodism was about was helping people grow in the knowledge and love of God.... And I think that has been endemic to the character of Methodism ever since...."

Pickens called the next witness, John McDermott, to testify as to whether or not Dell's ministry had an impact on the people where he lives and serves (Lakeview). McDermott was the Executive Director of the Lakeview Action Coalition, an organization made up of 32 institutions, including congregations, social service agencies and businesses in Lakeview. This community has a large gay and lesbian business district and residential population and, thus, places a great value on diversity. The year before, Dell had been elected to the coalition's Executive Committee.

McDermott testified about Dell's support for transitional housing for homeless women and affordable housing for senior citizens in the community.

He cited how, when Fred Phelps had come with his picketers

to Broadway Church the previous November, 450 people from the community attended the church's answer to his presence— an interfaith service against hate. These folks included a wide variety of clergy, including Roman Catholic, Lutheran, Jewish, United Church of Christ and others. Their presence demonstrated their commitment to peacemaking as well as their high esteem for Dell.

Elizabeth Cutter, who had turned 16 four days earlier, was the final witness for the day. Dell had been her pastor at Euclid Avenue UMC. A pretty, shy young girl with a sprinkle of freckles across her nose, Cutter was frightened but in control. She testified in her quiet voice about her pastor's strong and effective leadership of the youth group.

"He's always taught me to be very accepting of people, to question things that were just told to me if they didn't seem quite right to me at first, and to always have confidence in myself and be true to myself.…

"He's also strengthened my belief in God a lot because when you're young, you don't really want to go to church. But I think a lot of [the] atmosphere that he created [showed me that he] really wanted me to come and learn more about God and keep going."

Pickens: "So he made you more interested in going to church?"

Cutter: "Yes."

Pickens: "And are you still quite active in the church?"

Cutter: "Yeah. I'm on staff parish and Christian ed and I do a lot of stuff with the kids."

Pickens: "So would you say that Greg had a big impact on how you are involved today in the church?"

Cutter: "Yes. I'm not sure that if I hadn't had a pastor as strong as him I would have continued to stay in the church this long."

Pickens: "OK, thank you. Did you write a poem about Greg?"

Cutter: "Yes. [Laughter.] I wrote it in eighth grade because we had to write tribute poems to someone who is like a hero to us and Greg's always been like that to me…. Okay. I'm just warning everyone I'm not a very good poet, so…." [Laughter.]

"For my old Pastor Greg who protested, and got arrested. Always had a smile on his face. Wasn't afraid to cry or comfort me. Never stood still and always worked. Knew all the answers and loved all the children.

"For my old Pastor Greg who … made me include everyone. He flew a plane and sailed boats and always had something nice to say. He loved chocolate and puppets, too. He couldn't carry a tune or keep a beat." [Laughter.]

Pickens: "He still can't." [Laughter.]

Cutter: "For my old Pastor Greg who in his yard I caught fireflies and played on the statue. He told me God wasn't a boy and taught me to respect myself and others, too…."

The court seemed moved by Elizabeth's earnestness. Having finished her testimony, she returned to her seat.

After a hymn and a prayer, Bishop Tuell announced that this would conclude the proceedings for this day. The trial would reconvene, he said, at 8:30 AM the following morning.

summer, 1976
naperville · illinois

One evening, a few weeks after Gary and I started seeing the marriage counselor, I stood at the kitchen stove in our three-bedroom, split-level, suburban home, stirring instant potatoes for a throw-together dinner for our hungry family. The potatoes smelled dry and unappealing. I had no time for real cooking since Gary and I had just returned from a difficult counseling session. I knew that the children, momentarily distracted by a TV program in the basement family room, wouldn't care how the food was prepared.

I warmed up leftover meatloaf and took the time to husk some ears of corn. They turned bright yellow as they bobbed around in the steaming pot of water. *At least the corn smells fresh*, I thought. Gary, polite but remote, set the table with our white Melmac dishes decorated with blue- and green-striped borders. Designed to take abuse, they remained unscarred after 15 years of marriage and looked crisp and clean. I, on the other hand, wilted in the summer heat and began to cry.

Gary walked over to the basement door to call the kids to dinner but hesitated when he noticed me sobbing. At first he just came and stood near me, his dark eyes both impatient and concerned as he looked at my tear-stained, contorted face. I'm not sure if he had ever seen me cry so hard, even when my sweet Grandmother Sellers died right after we moved to the Midwest, and we couldn't afford for me to return to Florida for her funeral.

He just stood there, shifting his weight from one foot to the other as if he didn't know what to do. I wished he would touch me, maybe put his hand reassuringly on my shoulder, but he didn't. He quietly asked, "What's wrong, Ermalou?"

I kept crying. I couldn't stop and I couldn't answer. I just kept stirring and struggling to breathe between great, wrenching sobs.

"Good grief, Ermalou, what is it?" he demanded.

Finally I caught my breath enough to speak. "I just can't imagine life without Chuck," I wailed. "It just doesn't feel fair that I have to quit seeing him to keep our marriage together." My grief felt so profound that I wanted Gary's sympathy and understanding. In some ways it seems outrageous to me now that I would have expected his compassion. But on one level it made sense. He had, after all, agreed to the relationship that had become so meaningful to me.

He couldn't have cared less. Or maybe he just felt relieved that our counselor had insisted on this move. I had acceded to the demand but now wondered if I could honor it. It hurt so much to even think about it, I just kept sobbing. My heart felt broken, and I realized that my grief over losing Chuck was too profound to dismiss lightly.

About a month later I dared to reconnect with Chuck over Gary's objections. I told my husband I would be willing to significantly limit my time with Chuck, but I would not totally end the relationship. After experiencing how full, exciting, joyful and mutually respectful a relationship could be, I knew that, just like my preparation for ministry, it was vital to who I was. I could no longer ignore either call in my life.

However, I also realized I had no guidelines to follow. I knew nothing else to do except to keep going and try to find my way, with God's help. But I wondered: *Is God there anymore for me or too disgusted with me to be present?* I had no clear answer, although it felt that something true, something real, was happening and that I must pay close attention.

Even as the threat of divorce loomed over us, I couldn't believe that such a thing would happen. We had built a life together for 15 years. Our children needed and loved both of us and vice versa. Surely my spiritual awakening, my call to ministry and even my experimental relationship with Chuck wouldn't destroy all this.

Gary met my fresh determination with quiet fortitude, which lulled me into thinking we were past immediate danger. After another week of calm, I let down my defenses and began celebrating the positives of my life. I felt fortunate and blessed about my call to pastoral ministry. As seminary life continued to progress, so did deep spiritual and emotional satisfaction. I had never dreamed that life could be so good. I felt more alive than ever before, continued to adore my precious children, felt kinder and more tolerant of my husband, relished my limited time with Chuck and loved God more than I thought possible. My energy seemed limitless and my joy profound.

I began singing the theme song, "It Feels Good," from my musical on my way to and from the seminary each day, reveling in my good fortune:

> It feels good showing the way I truly feel.
> It feels good getting in touch with what is real.
> It feels good knowing that it's OK to be,
> Whatever the heck is honestly, authentically me.
> (Refrain) It's so good I want to share it.
> Come on folks, why don't you dare it?
> It feels good, oh my, does it feel good!
>
> It feels good letting the teardrops finally show.
> It feels good feeling that inside tension go.
> It feels good not solving all the problems myself,
> And taking those old feelings right off of the shelf.
> (Refrain) It's so good I want to share it.
> Come on folks, why don't you dare it?
> It feels good, oh my, does it feel good!

"It Feels Good." Ermalou M. Roller, 1976.

Then Gary made a confession to me. We were attending a weekend marriage enrichment retreat with a dozen other people from the church. The leaders of the retreat promised we could improve good marriages and repair shaky ones by honing our communication skills. This possibility seemed tailor-made for us. Perhaps we would find a way to fix us, I thought.

We arrived at the nearby Roman Catholic retreat center about 10:00 AM on Sunday, planning to stay for two nights. The center appeared to be antiseptically clean and sparsely furnished, adequate if not comfortable. Every wall had a carving of Jesus hanging on the cross. As United Methodists we celebrate the empty cross signifying a risen Christ. Seeing so many crosses with a crucified

Jesus on the walls became a reason for many of us to giggle. No one wanted to admit it, but we all felt slightly nervous.

The retreat leaders greeted each of us warmly as we arrived and announced that the program would begin in half an hour. We were to assemble in the large group room, furnished with folding chairs arranged in a circle. The other rooms facing this space would be used for private sessions with our spouses. We put our luggage in the bedrooms a short walk down a hall, past the cafeteria where we would eat our meals, and gathered to begin.

Soon after the program started, the leader assigned a couple's exercise. Gary and I found a small break-off room with two folding chairs facing one another and a small table in between. The prerequisite figure of the crucified Jesus hung on the wall. We sat down and put our notebooks on the table. As I looked at the written instructions for our assignment, Gary interrupted.

"Ermalou, there's something I've wanted to tell you for a long time," he said.

I glanced up and saw that he looked frightened. Puzzled and alarmed, I reached for his hands. "What is it, honey?"

"This is hard to say, so I'm just going to get it out," he said.

But then he didn't. Instead he looked at me sadly then back down at his hands. Pulling them away from mine, he gripped each side of the small table. He paused for what seemed like a very long time. His thumbnails turned white from pressure and his jaw moved back and forth. I began wondering what horrible trauma might warrant his strained silence. Was he going to ask for a divorce? Was he seriously ill? But neither idea came anywhere close and, in fact, no matter how much time might have elapsed, I would never have guessed what came next. Finally, he looked up at me and quietly spoke his truth.

"Ermalou, I'm gay."

I shall never forget how the light went out of his large brown eyes as he spoke those words. Usually lively, they suddenly seemed dead, as if an invisible switch had been clicked off. I've never seen anything like it before or since. I felt stunned into silence—both by his words and by what seemed like death looking at me. And, God help us, a kind of death did stare me in the face. All I could do was stare back at him with a blank expression, feeling confusion and disbelief.

The silence grew heavy between us. It took great effort to gather myself up after feeling his pronouncement as a stunning physical blow out of nowhere. After a while, I finally spoke.

"How long have you known this, Gary?"

"Since childhood," he answered sadly. "I've known for a very long time."

"Why didn't you tell me before now?" I asked sympathetically.

"I was afraid to," he said. "I was afraid it would be the end of us."

Had logic been ruling the day, I would have then asked a multitude of questions: Why did you marry me knowing this? Did you ever really love me? Do you now? Is this why you were willing to go along with the open marriage experiment? What does this mean about our children? Is this inherited? What do we do now?

But I didn't ask these questions because logic didn't motivate me at that moment. Love did. I said, "It will be all right, honey. We'll find a way to work this out."

I reached for Gary and held him tightly in my arms, trying to console him about all the pain he had felt for so many years. I also desperately wanted to feel the touch of something solid. Reality had just become exposed as illusion. Fifteen years of illusion.

My mind raced. The underlying basis for so many of our conflicts became clear: Subtle dissatisfactions and deep confusion were now legitimate; my instinct about something being very wrong in my life had been heartbreakingly correct; my exhilarating experience with Chuck now made even more sense.

Too overwhelmed to think anymore, I succumbed to the power of the moment. We sat holding each other for a long time. I'm not sure, but I think he cried. All I can remember from that point on is feeling a tight pressure in my chest. The tiny room became crowded and airless, as if we'd just been in a car wreck and an air bag had smashed us up against one another. I half expected to hear the door collapse outward and crash to the floor. But nothing moved. There was only silence. Silence and that crucified Jesus, with outstretched arms, looking down at us.

Somehow we managed to get through the rest of the retreat. We both felt too emotionally exhausted to talk on the way home. For the next few days I did what I often do: I dealt with my own shock, grief and anger by supplanting them with more constructive emotions. I tried to understand and feel sympathetic about his plight. I naively thought that now that we both knew the truth about his sexual orientation, we could work out our issues and hold our marriage together.

We had a lot to work out. In today's world, this expectation seems unrealistic at best. Then, however, divorce just wasn't an option for most people. In fact, polite society found it highly unacceptable. Women understood that, no matter what, they were to stand by their man, which meant they would stay married until one of the marriage partners died. I had not broken from that early strong teaching. In addition, most people didn't discuss or understand homosexuality in any kind of rational or scientific fashion. As is no doubt obvious, I remained personally clueless about it at the time.

Nonetheless, my head spun with ideas. Given our culture's condemnation of his orientation, I thought that Gary could have married me in an attempt to be "normal." Perhaps he simply wanted children and thought he could provide enough of my needs to give me a fair bargain. Maybe he really had fallen in love with me and thought that by acting on that feeling he could deny or at least minimize his true sexual needs.

For a few days after the retreat, I wondered why compassion wouldn't have urged him to tell me his secret when he saw me struggling with my own agonizing life questions. No wonder he felt afraid of my relationship with Chuck. Had I realized what existed under the surface of our marriage, I would have been afraid of it too.

Yet I also remembered how dangerous it was to be gay when we were growing up. People not only ridiculed gays and lesbians, but they also jailed them for what they labeled deviant behavior, even when that behavior had been with another consenting adult. Condemned by both church and culture, called disparaging names, made the subjects of vicious jokes and the recipients of physical violence, homosexuals learned very early in their lives to be afraid and to guard their secret carefully.

How awful, I thought, to be forced to live a lie, to never be able to enter into an honest relationship that society celebrated with gift showers, newspaper announcements and congratulations all around. How sad to find out as a child you were basically unacceptable unless you pretended to be something you weren't. How lucky I had been to be able to openly protest the female stereotypes our culture had tried to force upon me; how dangerous it would have been for him to do the same thing.

His confession forced me to think about this world that I knew little about. I had participated in denigrating it enough, however, to recognize how painful it must be to be homosexual. Nonetheless, I needed to know the answers to my many questions. I felt a deep sense of rejection and a lot of confusion. I even felt shame, thinking that somehow Gary's revelation about himself meant that something was terribly wrong with me because I had married him. I felt trapped with him in the pain of needing to live with this big secret in order to protect our children and avoid society's judgmental attitudes about his authentic identity.

Yet I remained certain that discussing this could lead to holding our marriage together. This fantasy lasted two weeks. Without answering my multitude of questions or working with me to figure a way through it, Gary refused to discuss the matter further.

"This is your problem," he told me. "Not mine."

CHAPTER SIX

Friday, March 26, 1999
downers grove · illinois

W hen the trial resumed on the second day, Bishop Tuell greeted those gathered, then announced that the Trial Court had not yet arrived due to bad traffic. He had the group sing a hymn and participate in a responsive reading for Christian unity from the hymnal. By the time this was finished, the jury had arrived and been seated.

Defense Counsel Pickens called James Walter Reed Jr. as the defense's first witness. An attorney, Reed was married and working as a political consultant. He had been an active lay member of Broadway UMC for seven years and was co-chair of the Committee on Religion and Race and a member of the Committee on Staff–Parish Relations.

He testified that he supported homosexual union services and expressed appreciation for the model of inclusiveness at the church. This attitude of inclusiveness, he said, "brings in extraordinary numbers of visitors every week and many of those who end up actually ... becoming members of the church."

He also testified about how Dell had been very instrumental "in creating a model that talked about not only having a core group of people but bringing those from the outside, sort of what we call our oasis members ... and making them more included in their own way.

"We know there were people ... who aren't necessarily part of the inside core that still want to participate and be a part of Broadway Church ... so he has enabled them to feel welcome...."

Terry Lynn Vanden Hoek, an emergency room physician at the University of Chicago, was called to the witness stand next. He had been reared in South Dakota as a member of the Christian Reformed Church and had been a member of Broadway UMC since 1996. He testified about his difficult personal journey growing up in a Christian Reformed Church and how the pastor had welcomed him to Broadway and helped him grow spiritually.

Pickens: "Now, I want to shift to your faith development at Broadway. And when you think about that ... what lengths did you go to in order to reconcile your love of the Christian faith and your personal feelings?"

Vanden Hoek: "It was a long and painful road I can only say.... one thing that I really appreciated about [the] United Methodist Church ... is that it's not just scripture. It's [also] tradition, experience and reason. And in the church I grew up in, it was scripture, scripture, scripture and scripture. And so I heard the stories of Sodom and Gomorrah. I heard that being gay is a terrible thing. Well, it's difficult to bring up the issue in that kind of context, it really is. And I really felt that I was bound and determined to, you know if that was the case, if that's what God's word was saying, that I needed to change. I mean, there's just no two ways about it. I believe the Bible.

"And so, you know, I prayed about it, morning, noon and night. I cried about it many times. I dated many women ... Almost got married to one ... we looked like a wonderful couple together. But it was a lie. That's also wrong in the church.

"So even though it would have been easier ... to be accepted by other people, I decided not to get married and continued to question whether—basically I had to leave the church.

"I don't think anyone realizes how lonely it is to grow up gay in the church. It is a very lonely experience because there are many people that say that you're supposed to love your neighbor as yourself. But they never once tried to get to know me as a neighbor, let alone a brother. And if they had bothered to check, they would have found that there was a person that very much … was loving his God and … was loving his neighbor as himself but needed some guidance and help.

"And because there was nobody there to really talk to, at some point I guess I felt like I could not change who I was and there was a point in my life where I tried to kill myself. And as a result of that, I had a cardiac arrest. My heart stopped for ten minutes. And for some reason, maybe it had to do with the fact that it was just after Easter, I came back. My parents were told that I'd probably have permanent brain damage as a result of what happened. And I still sometimes wonder if I did. [Laughter.] It is a great handicap if I need to have it.

"But that is the extent to which I went to change who I was. To go to the grave itself. And I can only tell you that it doesn't work. I went to Moody Bible Church for a whole day to hear about ex-gay ministries and about changing your sexuality, and I gave it a lot of consideration. I talked to people. I went to evening sessions that met. And I came to a conclusion that these people were leading lies. They were living them out and I knew it because I had done it. I'd seen it. I know how to put on a good show. And that's what I was seeing.

"And as I got to know other people who had accepted their sexuality and were leading normal lives, I came to the conclusion that it is possible to be Christian and … gay….

"Greg Dell pointed out some things about, well, what do United Methodists believe? And … that's not an easy question since United Methodists don't agree on all aspects of doctrine. And Greg Dell pointed out that this is a pretty argumentative bunch. And he said you're probably going to meet some people you don't like. And he's right. I did. [Laughter.]

"But the other thing he gave me was the Social Principles. And we spent some time talking about these. And I even highlighted the stuff from back then. A couple things I was impressed with … 'The Social Principles are a call to all members of the United Methodist Church to a prayerful, studied dialogue of faith and practice.' And I was impressed that the Methodists were interested in a discussion with me. They were interested in hearing what I had to say. That people weren't going to cut off our conversation prematurely. That they were going to get to know who I was.

"I don't know about any of you, but I think that living for the rest of your life alone is a hard thing to ask anybody. And we're not talking just about sex. I mean, we're talking about going out to the movies together with somebody that you like … knowing that somebody likes a lot of ketchup with their fries … knowing that somebody likes cream and sugar in their coffee … visiting somebody when they get sick … wondering what's going to happen when you get old. Am I going to be by myself, or am I going to be with a partner who's really going to care about who I am?

"That's one of the things that my dad taught me as well. One night when we were building a pool back in the backyard, he was using the belt sander and once in a while he would stop and we'd just kind of talk about things. And it was just one of those little moments that come up once in a while where you kind of realize, wow, I really have a cool dad. And he said, you know, Terry, there's going to be a lot of decisions that you make, and I'm really proud of what you've done so far. But one thing that is just absolutely critical is to choose your right partner. Because, bottom line is, that's going to be the one that really cares the most about you in life and who's going to care when you get sick and who's going to, you know, care about you when you get older. So choose well. Choose well."

Karl Reinhardt, whom Dell had joined with Keith Eccarius in a union service, testified next. Reinhardt is a high school teacher who had been reared in the Missouri Synod of the

Lutheran Church. His father is a retired LMS pastor.

"We went through seven or eight counseling sessions, the planning sessions, and those started in August or September of '97."

Pickens: "So your counseling sessions were the same as … the ones that he [Dell] does for heterosexual[s]?"

Reinhardt: "Right. That he does for all couples, yes."

Pickens: "What was your family's reaction to your deciding to have a holy union service?"

Reinhardt: "They were happy for us because they had met Keith several times. They liked Keith. They could see that we were a real couple in every sense of the word.

"I had asked my dad if he wanted to participate in the ceremony…. He said … that for professional reasons he did not think that it would be appropriate…. I did not find that offensive in any way…. He wound up … giving the prayer at the reception…."

Pickens then asked why Reinhardt wanted to enter into a holy covenant.

Reinhardt: "Quite simply, we love each other. We want to spend the rest of our lives with each other in a monogamous relationship."

Pickens: "What was the significance of the holy union service in your relationship?"

Reinhardt: "It was significant … To make a firm witness about our relationship in an atmosphere that was so important to both of us, which is the church, in front of our family … friends … in front of our God…."

Keith Eccarius, Reinhardt's partner, testified next. Eccarius grew up in Chicago and is a systems analyst. He had been a member at Broadway for eight years.

Pickens: "And what was your first religious affiliation?"

Eccarius: "When I was a teenager, I started going to an Assembly of God Church Sunday School and friends in the neighborhood started taking me there and I got more and more involved and stayed with that church until I came out."

Pickens: "OK. What was it that appealed to you about that church?"

Eccarius: "It was a sense of community that I had not experienced at home. It was my love of music. It was a place that I could go and sing."

Pickens: "What happened when that congregation learned about your being gay?"

Eccarius: "I was asked to leave."

Pickens: "What was your response to Pastor Dell's counseling sessions?"

Eccarius: "It was very thorough. And what struck me most is that no couple could go through this series of sessions and come out not knowing what the commitment meant that they were getting involved in."

Pickens: "Would you say that it helped you—that they helped you think through your commitment?"

Eccarius: "Definitely…."

summer, 1976
naperville · illinois

Eventually, I accepted the fact that my marriage to Gary couldn't last. The unspoken choice—the only choice—Gary seemed to offer me was to close the lid on my questions, as well as my newfound sense of liberation, and go along with our charade of a marriage or divorce him. I knew immediately that I couldn't join him in stuffing my feelings and pretending that things were OK. He had more experience at doing that—and apparently more incentive to continue, no matter the cost to both of us, our family and the community at large. That community continues to function as if homosexuals never marry straight spouses. It often ignores the resulting problems when they do, and it doesn't acknowledge how society contributes to this state of affairs. I sadly chose divorce, assuming we would agree to joint custody of our children. I was wrong.

Gary's amenable personality changed dramatically, and he sought full custody. His anger knew no reasonable bounds. He attacked me verbally on a regular basis. He shocked both our joint attorney and me when he expressed his strong conviction that I should never again be permitted to be in our children's presence.

Gary should have known he didn't have to take this aggressive stance since I would never ban him from being with our children. Later I wondered if he simply used me as a convenient scapegoat, loading me up with his long suppressed if understandable rage about having to hide his true identity.

Or perhaps fear of exposure controlled him, making him think that by lashing out at me, he might save his reputation in the community, his business, his relationship with his children and our extended families. He never asked if I would expose his sexual preference and I, mistakenly, just assumed he knew I wouldn't think of doing so.

He also might have realized what I didn't: that neither of us could predict what the court would order. In some states this continues to be a threat to homosexuals. Our attorney warned me of the obvious: Gary had become vindictive toward me—more vindictive, he said, than anyone he had ever represented.

Frightened, hurt and confused, I privately sought out sources of help without Gary's knowledge. I talked with a psychologist on the seminary staff and consulted a female attorney. I thought that, should this come to a court fight, I would be awarded custody, as the mother almost always is. I expected this opinion to be validated, giving me leverage for achieving some reasonable agreement with Gary to share joint custody.

Both advisers shocked me by saying that, most likely, neither of us would have the support of a judge. In a court fight, Gary's sexual identity would have to be disclosed, which would prevent him from being granted custody. And I might not gain custody for other reasons:

First, I had embarked upon paths society did not recognize as valid by beginning seminary training as a woman and by deepening my relationship with Chuck (a fact that Gary quickly exploited).

Second, I had no income to support the children.

Third, knowing that our children needed both parents, I refused to divulge my estranged husband's sexual orientation to gain advantage over him. This would have jeopardized our children's relationship with their father. I knew what it meant to lose your dad. I wouldn't let that happen to our little ones.

I felt cornered, however, when they told me that, should I fight my husband for custody and lose, our children would be placed in foster care. Already in Detroit, Michigan, there had been a ruling that drew national attention against law student Jennifer Ireland. For a time she lost custody of her children because she used day care for her child while attending classes. It didn't seem relevant to the judge that the father worked all day and would also need someone else to care for their child. The ruling set off protests from groups including the American Civil Liberties Union and the National Organization for Women. After a two-year court battle, the original ruling was overturned.

However, given that first decision and similar court decisions that followed, and given my husband's determination to fight, my advisers convinced me that maternal custody would not be guaranteed. The custody battle would be long, arduous and expensive. We would not be able to choose the judge. Anything could happen.

Defeat swept over me when I realized that I could never put

our children through such a bitter fight, much less take the risk of causing them to lose their parents altogether.

The story in 1 Kings 3:22 (NRSV) of two women fighting over a child stuck in my mind. Both claimed to be the valid parent. The judge, King Solomon, suggested that justice would be served by cutting the child in two, giving one half to each person. Horrified, the true mother immediately agreed to give the child to the other woman.

I faced the reality that fighting for custody of the children would cause them great harm. So I took the bullet aimed at my heart, even as my spirit bowed low from heavy grief. I acceded to my husband's unfair and unreasonable demand. The earlier fear of stepping out of the cultural box was realized, and it felt as crushing as my intuition had warned me it would be.

Gary forced me to accept that I would be with the children only on weekends and holidays. This decision felt devastating for them and for me. Further, I became the first in my family to divorce. My mother took it very hard. Although she would reverse her decision the next year, and we would continue a wonderful relationship, she emotionally disinherited me at the time. Saying I had broken her heart and shamed the family, she withdrew her love and all contact. My sisters and brothers offered similar cold shoulders, some through their silence and others through their judgmental questions. Later they would also reunite with me. At the time, however, the absence of their support was agonizing. I felt particularly offended by the most ironic and cutting question one asked of me: "How can you *leave* your children?" The feelings of abandonment I must have had as a child when my dad died returned with a vengeance. My mom, brothers and sisters disappeared—again.

That first time when my mother and siblings "deserted" me due to practical necessity, I must have blamed myself. This is, at least, what psychologists tell us about how young children make sense of such events. This time, when my mother and siblings elected to desert me, it hurt more than ever. Even though Gary had told them his side of the story (that I had engaged in an "affair," leaving out that he had agreed to the open marriage and that he is gay), it still felt unwise for me to disclose his sexual orientation and all of the other private details that led to the divorce decision. Of course, knowing the truth would have helped them understand and offer me support. Yet I wanted them to trust in me and in my integrity based on their life-long experience with me. They clearly communicated that they did not and that they blamed me totally. This time, the condemnation was neither self-imposed nor imagined.

December 20, 1976, is a day I shall never forget. One day before my 37th birthday, I loaded up my belongings in my car and drove from our home in suburbia to my small rented city apartment in Rogers Park near the seminary. The eerie coincidence of my age being the same as that of my father when he had left one life for the next didn't occur to me; neither did the coincidence of a broadcast news report I heard on the way to my apartment. Halfway there, a radio announcer shared a bulletin that Richard J. Daley, the powerful and controversial mayor of Chicago, had died suddenly of an apparent heart attack, as suddenly as my father had died.

Many in the city shared my overwhelming feelings, conscious and unconscious, of being lost, frightened, grief-stricken, confused, heartbroken and lonely. I carried the additional crushing burdens of shame and failure. I realized that my car already led a funeral procession, not for Mayor Daley, but for me.

I had died to a long-held identity, leaving my home and my marriage, reluctantly settling for seeing Stan, Kathy and Mike on weekends. I had chosen to temporarily endure the sting of condemnation and abandonment by my family of origin rather than risk my mother and siblings doing the same, in a permanent way, to my children's father. I could no longer be associated with the adult class that had inadvertently exploded the wall of safety I had built around myself. I was also physically moving away from Chuck. He continued to provide emotional support, but I wondered how often he could drive the nearly 80-mile round trip to see me. The 37-year-old spirit child hiding within felt exposed—naked and frightened, hungry and hopeful, tender and lost.

I tentatively took the extended hand of God to be led into the mysterious process of growing up called "transformation." Liturgically speaking, I began moving out of the darkness of Lent and into the light of Easter. Even though the sting and stench of death surrounded me, I felt the undeniable presence, love and forgiveness of God, who tenderly yet firmly encouraged me to take my second baby step into a new reality. God's Spirit helped me grieve the death of my ego-constructed self who worshipped the safety of cultural conformity. I had given this up in order to embrace the fullness of a new life. This new life would be shaped and controlled, led and commissioned by God. For what? Only God knew.

▲ 1961: My brother
Edward (a.k.a Ralph)
McDuffie ready to
"give me away"
to Gary

▶ 1965: With Stan and
baby Kathy

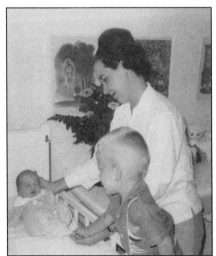

▲ 1969: Stan, Mike and Kathy
(photo by Cliff McDuffie)

➤ 1972: The kids at Christmas

▼ 1977: Celebrating with Kathy,
who was playing for the first
gender-mixed ball team in
Naperville, Illinois

◀ 1977: My ordination by Bishop Paul Washburn

▼ 1978: Skip Ellzey and Penny Penrose with Chuck and me on our wedding day

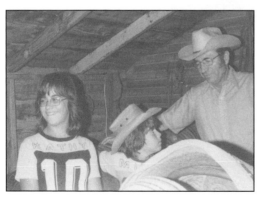

◀ 1979: Kathy, Mike and Chuck in the Saddle House at the LZ Ranch

▲ 1980: With Mike at a birthday dinner

◀ 1980: Holding a rattler at the LZ Ranch with Stan looking on

▲ 2009: Greg Dell *(courtesy of Josh Hawkins/Wednesday Journal)*
▼ 2009: Dell responding after receiving the Gilbert H. Caldwell
Justice Ministry Award *(courtesy of Church Within A Church)*

CHAPTER SEVEN

Friday, March 26, 1999
downers grove · illinois

After a ten-minute recess, Greg Dell climbed the stairs to the lone open chair as the last witness for the trial.

He was asked to spell out his education (BA from Illinois Western University and MDiv from Duke Divinity School), and he answered questions about his considerable service to the general church. He explained that after his ordination in 1969 he served as pastor in Minooka, Evanston, Oak Park, and now at Broadway. He had attended the last five General Conferences as an observer and active participant in working with delegates and sharing information. And he had been an alternate delegate to the last General Conference and a delegate to the Jurisdictional Conference. He was a member of the General Commission on Religion and Race, served on its Executive Committee and chaired its Planning and Evaluation Committee for the General Commission. He also served on the Jurisdictional Commission on Religion and Race and was the financial secretary of its Executive Committee.

Defense Counsel Pickens: "What are the differences when you think about the whole spectrum of your ministry? What's your experience?"

Dell: "Well, I think that the differences focus on what people bring as they come to meet God and when they come to meet the church. What are their experiences? How has God spoken through their lives already? What has the church said to them already in their lives, and what are they looking to do? How are they ...

intending to connect and to work out their ministry now in that particular place? So each setting, depending on the congregation, is going to require some different sensitivities."

Pickens: "Do you see any unifying themes?"

Dell: "Yes. I think people are looking to meet God. I think there's a spiritual hunger throughout all the communities I've served. I think people are looking for a passionate, vital faith, one that's relevant and real for their lives. My experience is most of the folks within my work are not interested in simply going to church because that's something to do. They have that spiritual hunger.

"I think the other unifying theme is that people really want to grow. And all of us are a little uncomfortable with challenge. But in the context of a loving community where it's safe to think and to ask and to explore … challenge is warmly welcome and we all grow."

Dell was then asked about the issue of the trial, specifically when he had agreed to do the union service, what he required of the gay couple, and whether or not he was aware that he was breaking church law by going ahead with the service after the Judicial Court ruling.

He responded with the facts about the counseling already verbalized by Reinhardt and Eccarius, which confirmed that he was fully aware of the new legislation.

"I was present at the General Conference in 1996 and … I was on the floor and, in fact, made a speech on the piece of legislation that was being proposed. So I was fully aware of the debate, participated in it personally along with the delegation from Northern Illinois, and our position did not prevail.

"We were aware immediately that the provision was placed in the Social Principles and at the very least, that created a situation of legal ambiguity since the Social Principles state explicitly in their preface that they are for the guidance and persuasion of the church in the best of the prophetic spirit. And we're all aware …

that you don't take that lightly. That's … not simply a statement of how we're feeling today. That's the position that the majority of the denomination has agreed to support on a whole range of issues of social justice and care for God's world. That is the position of the church. But it is through persuasion and guidance."

Dell went on to explain that a movement called "In All Things Charity" had been formed as a response to this ruling. It provided an opportunity for both clergy and laity to make a statement of conscience. "Basically," he said, "…[it was] a statement indicating that those who signed that statement were in opposition … to the position that the church was taking in regard to a wide range of issues in regard to sexual orientation, all of those positions being negative positions the church had taken…. We had over 1,300 clergy persons indicate their support…."

He then reviewed the trial of Rev. Jimmy Creech, a longtime friend of his from Duke Divinity School. Creech was tried for, but not convicted of, disobeying the *Discipline*, since officiating at union services was discouraged but not yet against church law. "Subsequent to that," Dell explained, "the Judicial Council was asked to consider a declaratory decision….

"In August of 1998, the Judicial Council gave a very clear decision that it was binding church law and as such that it would subject anyone who violated that … to a charge of disobedience to the order and discipline of the church.

"When I became aware of that, I not only spoke with Karl and Keith about their service, but met with a group of clergy in Northern Illinois who had been conducting services of holy union and suggested in that context that I didn't think a trial would serve our interest in changing that rule very well and that it was my opinion that if we could focus our energies instead on working toward General Conference and on educating and sharing our stories, that that would be the most appropriate way to address what I felt, and I think those in that room that day felt, was an injustice.

"I also suggested ... that a number of us had services planned and would be conducting services and we needed to make decisions as pastors about how we would proceed. It was in that context that I talked with Karl and Keith and ... decided to go ahead with the service...."

Pickens: "Why?"

Dell: "Because I didn't feel that I was being disobedient to the order and discipline of the United Methodist Church. On the contrary, I felt that the only way I could be obedient would be to conduct that service.

"Specifically, there was a rule that said I could not extend a particular kind of ministry to the people whom I was serving. I'd been appointed to Broadway to serve all those people. Black and white and brown and yellow, male and female, about half of each, younger congregation, and about 30 percent gay or lesbian. That was the percentage when I arrived at Broadway in 1995. That's about the percentage it is now.

"And the church said to me, through my vow—from the time ... of my ordination ... until I was appointed at Broadway ... you go out there and you be a pastor. You bring word, order and sacrament. You preach, you teach, you order the life of the church so that it's consistent with who we are as United Methodists and our understanding of how we make decisions and how we function together. You practice the sacraments faithfully ... You relate to the people as the servant leader ... You baptize all the people of God ... when ... they're ready for baptisms ... you confirm ... You bring people into membership. You invite them not just to join an institution but to be disciples. Be with them when they're hurt, and celebrate when their lives are full of joy. And when they die, bury them. Celebrate their lives. And one other thing. When they bring to you a relationship that is filled with love and commitment that understands the mystery of God in the midst of that love and commitment and they say to you, we want to offer that relationship as part of our ministry, we want the blessing of God and the church for that relationship, you do that as a privilege as a pastor.

"And then in 1996, the church said for everybody except 30 percent of your church. Don't do it for them. It doesn't matter how deeply they love God. It doesn't matter how long they've been part of the church. It doesn't matter how healthy, fulfilling, responsible their relationship is. You can't do it for them….

"I know a lot about this book [indicating the *Discipline*]…. It means a lot to me. So does an even greater book than this. But I don't worship this book. And I don't worship the other one. I worship the God who I believe is behind … both books. That is to say, and maybe this would be the way to finish my response to you, I want to be a pastor. I think I am. I believe I'm a pastor obedient to the order and discipline of the church in terms of the very core of what it means to be a pastor. I make mistakes. I don't think I did when I celebrated this service. If I can't be a pastor fully to all the people to whom I'm appointed, you don't want me as a pastor. You really don't…."

During the cross-examination, Williams asked Dell: "Do you think you abused the United Methodist Church, its privileges it conferred on you at your ordination by this act of disobedience?"

Dell: "No, I think I honored it."

Williams: "Thank you."

From those gathered in the room came a chorus of "Amen."

As usual, the Trial Court members were permitted to ask questions of the witness. When this was completed and after a five-minute break, both Pickens and Williams made brief closing arguments.

Bishop Tuell then provided a form for the Trial Court to use in reporting their verdict. He reminded them, "that the standard of proof that the *Discipline* puts forth is clear and convincing evidence" and dismissed them to deliberate. It would take nine votes to return a verdict of guilty. If that happened, the penalty phase of the trial would begin immediately. If Dell was declared innocent, the trial would be concluded. Tuell commented that the trial would not reconvene until the Trial Court was ready with its verdict—a decision that probably would not come until after lunchtime.

He then declared the trial in recess.

spring, 1977
evanston · illinois

At seminary, Dr. Hessert listened to my story about losing custody of my children and encouraged me to accept that, although I was no longer a full-time mother to them, I was an important presence in their lives. Although the pain of their absence was unrelenting, I accepted his wisdom. One weekend, I observed it in action when Michael and I shopped for groceries. Like most eight-year-olds, he spotted things he hoped I would buy for him, and he lobbied for them. I had nearly finished shopping when my cart passed a sweets section, catching Mike's full attention. Quickly surveying the merchandise, he grabbed an item and started in on me.

"Mom, will you plea-ee-eese get this candy bar for me?" he asked.

"I'm sorry, Mike, but we already have candy in the shopping cart. I can't buy any more right now."

Astonished, he looked up at me with wide eyes. Misinterpreting his expression, I felt guilt rising up. I had worked hard to keep it at bay, resisting the temptation to placate my children with gifts to ward off their pain and my sadness about our weekday absence from one another. This time the struggle dissolved as Mike finally spoke, "Gee, Mom, you said that so *softly*!"

I smiled as I felt gratitude push out the guilt. Then I reached over and hugged him.

Contrary to my fears, Chuck and I continued to see one another throughout my seminary years, and I felt clear that I loved him. Mom had been right, if sketchy, in her advice that, "Nobody will have to tell you when you're really in love." Our passion seemed insatiable. Our joy in seeing one another and talking, playing and laughing together never failed.

Meanwhile, Chuck had separated from Marge, and I hoped we would marry after my divorce from Gary became final. But although he openly and clearly professed his love for me, Chuck didn't assume that marrying me would be wise. In spite of my pastoral care training, I remained ever the romantic who thought *our* love could overcome all obstacles. However, his life experience and wisdom told him that no matter how much we cherished one another, we must seriously deal with the 16-year difference in our ages, our distinct life experiences and our individual hopes for the future. We both knew that should we marry, we would also have to work hard to form a new family with his three adult children and my three young ones.

I understood these concerns and respectfully worked with him to sort them through. In spite of my feelings, or perhaps because of my love for him, I also encouraged him to return to Marge to explore whether they still had a chance to make a go of their marriage. I knew he deeply appreciated her, had a long history and three children with her and he wished to remain friends. To make this effort more legitimate, I suggested another time of separation between the two of us and he agreed.

I agonized during that time, but in my heart I felt this to be a wise move and one that would, ultimately, be best for us all, regardless of how it turned out. Chuck returned about a month later to say their reunion hadn't worked for either of them. They divorced not long afterward.

During my final six months at the seminary, I told Chuck he would soon have to decide about us. I felt that our social experiment had been legitimate, but I didn't want to bring it into my parish life. He decided to take time off to make up his mind. He figured that the best setting for such contemplation was the Ellzey Ranch near Perryton, Texas, where he had grown up and spent summers most of his life. So he left town for a time of personal reflection and self-care. Ten days later he called to say he would be coming home the next day and wanted to meet with me.

When I finished with my classes the following day, I rushed home to wash my hair and dress carefully for his visit. I chose a green knit pantsuit he had admired, wondering if I was preparing for the beginning of our engagement or the end of our relationship. I nervously dropped my liquid facial foundation into the sink, shattering the bottle, then had to wipe up the makeup around the shards of glass. I finished 15 minutes before he was to arrive and spent the time rearranging pillows on the sofa and doing other mundane tasks in my already-cleaned-for-the-occasion apartment.

Finally the buzzer sounded. I hit the "enter" button and waited impatiently for the elevator to bring him to my door. I quickly opened it when I heard his knock and saw a happy and confident man with a smile on his face and a bouquet of fresh flowers in his hands. Although it was difficult to ever predict what Chuck would do at any given time, I could tell right away it would be a happy evening.

When he presented me with a diamond ring that night, I joyfully accepted his proposal but refused the ring. "I've been there and done that," I said. Then I gently explained why this cultural expectation had little meaning for me anymore. I knew he couldn't afford a ring right then, and I had heard about an attractive alternative idea from a seminary classmate. A local jeweler was selling simple distressed gold bands that smoothed out more with every passing year. Soon after, he purchased two of the gold bands—one for each of us to wear as wedding rings when the time came.

summer, 1978
waukegan · illinois

Beginning in June 1978, my life changed dramatically yet again as I completed all but one course at the seminary and began serving as pastor of York House United Methodist Church near Waukegan, in northern Illinois near the Wisconsin border. I finished my studies, commuting to a class that met two nights a week, then waited to graduate the following year. Meanwhile, I began learning the names and stories of my 124 parishioners, finding my way around a largely rural community, discovering the practical side of parish ministry and learning to live without the day-to-day support of seminary friends.

I loved preaching every week but felt nervous about doing a decent job of it. Of course, I didn't want my congregation to know this and judge me to be inadequate. In fact I was inadequate. I would come to understand and accept that we clergy—from an experienced pastor speaking from a high pulpit in a grand cathedral to a frightened greenhorn speaking from a modest pulpit in a tiny country church—are all inadequate. We are all inadequate because the message we are called on to share is deeply personal in life-changing ways and, at the same time, so immense and beyond our full understanding as to be ineffable, especially in 20-minute sermons delivered to groups of half-attentive people.

My congregants were, of course, as caught up in their own issues as I was in mine. Still, we shared to some degree a common spiritual hunger to know Truth, Love, Good Parent, Source of Life, Spirit—the "I am who I am" God we are even too inadequate to sufficiently name.

We met for worship every Sunday morning in the small historic space that seemed more like a chapel than a sanctuary. Only 80 people could fit in the century-old structure at one time, and the wood floors shook when that kind of "crowd" came. Usually we numbered 35 or so. Elegant furnishings that had seen better days shared the space with simple, unsophisticated art. Behind the pulpit sat the high-backed, intricately carved wooden pastor's chair, which had a dusty brocade-covered seat so loose I feared falling through it. A paint-by-number picture of Jesus and felt banners in bold colors hung on the front walls. Along the sides of the sanctuary, light filtered in through windows with simple shapes of colored glass. Yet we all accepted this organic blend. It was the best the congregation could do, and the mix honestly reflected who we were.

We all came to the service trusting, or at least hoping, that something might be said worth listening to, that something might be served up in the gathered community as we grappled with ourselves, with one another, with scripture and with the Great Other. In short, we hoped for something that would nourish us, giving us that which we cannot provide for ourselves.

I had finalized my divorce from Gary by the time I went to York House, but my move from Rogers Park to Waukegan presented new family challenges. Stan, Kathy and Mike had longer to travel since Waukegan was farther from Naperville than Rogers Park (a difference of 15 miles each way). Riding the train was no longer feasible, which meant they spent at least two hours every weekend in a car. Fortunately, Stan had earned his driver's license a month before my appointment to the church, so he helped with some of the driving, as did Gary. But no one could shave time from the long commute. In addition, when they were with me, the kids missed free time with their friends.

I began to realize how lonely and abused good fathers must feel who divorce and lose custody of their children. I mused that, since I sought to do "a man's job," some would think it poetic justice that I know a divorced man's pain. I became sensitized to it, but while I endured my personal pain, my children's anguish and confusion nearly did me in.

Fortunately, weekends with my children weren't totally bleak. We managed to have some good and meaningful times together in spite of the circumstances. I traveled to Naperville to see their school programs. At my parsonage we celebrated birthdays, strung popcorn for the Christmas tree, sang songs together and continued other traditions.

Already kind human beings, most of the time they did their best to make me happy even as I did the same for them. We knew we loved one another, but pain continued to be a strong, mostly silent enemy. Mike, Kathy and Stan were too young to initiate discussions about their feelings, although Kathy acted out some of hers. And I had lost so much of my cherished role as their mother that I wanted to spend the little time we had together protecting and building up what was positive between us.

I realized that if the children could have talked about their feelings of being "abandoned" by me, they could have healed more quickly. But their father's support was essential for those discussions to happen, and I knew that I wouldn't have it. Although he had initially responded positively to my request for family therapy, he withdrew himself and our children after a few sessions when, as the therapist told me, "It began actually working."

So I did the best I could to create safe, positive memories with them and to trust that God's grace would prevail for all of us.

Author and poet John Shea helped immensely in this spiritual struggle, especially with his poem "A Prayer to the God Who Fell From Heaven," from his book *The God Who Fell From Heaven*. I included the poem in sermons more than once; and it is reprinted here with permission from the author.

If you had stayed
tightfisted in the sky
and watched us thrash
with all the patience of a pipe smoker,
I would pray
like a golden bullet aimed at your heart.
But the story says
you cried
and so heavy was the tear
you fell with it to earth
where like a baritone in a bar
it is never time to go home.
So you moved among us
twisting every straight line
into Picasso,
stealing kisses from pinched lips,
holding our hand in the dark.
So now when I pray
I sit and turn my mind
like a television knob
till you are there
with your large, open hands
spreading my life before me
like a Sunday tablecloth
and pulling up a chair yourself
for by now
the secret is out.
You are home.

CHAPTER EIGHT

Hours passed while the Trial Court deliberated. Finally the members slowly filed back into the hushed room.

Bishop Tuell: "We're now ready to resume our proceedings and the Trial Court is here and do you have a chairperson?"

Trial Court Chairperson: "Yes, sir."

Tuell: "Would you stand? Have you reached a verdict?"

Trial Court Chairperson: "Yes, we have."

Tuell: "All right. I want to ask you to hand the verdict form to the bailiff who will give it to the Secretary. And before it is read, I'd like to share with you this statement: I do not know what this verdict is. I have no idea at all. Whatever it is, however, I know that this verdict for some will be a source of great joy while for others it may be a source of pain and anguish. We are the church gathered. We are, in the language of scripture, the body of Christ. Therefore, in consideration of those for whom whatever verdict may cause pain, I ask you to continue your refrain from expressions of assent or disapproval, whatever the verdict.

"There are those who are saying our church will divide over this issue in this case. I do not believe this. But our conduct today can be a powerful symbol that the body of Christ will not be rent.

"Will you help me in this?"

He was answered with a chorus of "Yes."

Bishop Tuell: "And will you reserve your personal expressions of feeling, which I know are very natural, until the final adjournment of this trial? Will you do that?"

More yeses.

Bishop Tuell: "Thank you." He then read the verdict.

"'As to the charge, disobedience to the order and discipline of the United Methodist Church, we the Trial Court find the Respondent guilty.' Ten votes were cast for guilty. Three votes were cast not guilty.

"'As to the specification that on or about September 19, 1998, Reverend Gregory Dell conducted the service between Mr. Eccarius and Mr. Reinhardt, the Trial Court finds the Respondent guilty.' Thirteen to nothing."

There were no cheers, no applause, no comment, just a collective gasp followed by the sound of quiet sobbing as people reached for one another's hands and embraced. Williams, with tears in his eyes, crossed the room to hug Greg Dell, who graciously received his gesture. Williams and others in the room must have felt vindicated by the verdict, but most of those present felt a heavy cloak of despair that nearly snuffed out all hope that our denomination would be a beacon of justice and grace-filled faith.

Outside in the parking lot, weary media people remained on alert, standing and waiting with the crowd to hear the verdict. It was now 4:30 PM, six and a half hours since the trial had begun that morning. But the court still had to proceed with the penalty phase, so no announcements were made to the media.

Tuell: "Now at this time, it becomes our duty to take up the next phase of this trial, the penalty phase."

Trial Court Chairperson: "Bishop?"

Tuell: "Yes."

Chairperson: "I wonder if the Trial Court might make a brief statement. Would this be the appropriate time or later?"

Tuell: "Yes, you may make a statement at this time unless there's objection from counsel."

Pickens: "No objection."

Williams: "No."

Chairperson: "The Trial Court struggled with the lack of a clear definition of what constitutes order and discipline of the church as it is constituted in paragraph 2624.1e. We feel without clarity around the definition of order and discipline and its implications, every future Trial Court will be forced to define those words before it does its work. Thank you."

Tuell: "All right, thank you. At this time, I don't know if … counsel would like to have a brief recess?"

Pickens: "That's fine."

Whereupon a five-minute recess was declared by Tuell for counsel, "to get your heads together and then we're going on to start on the next phase of the trial."

Bishop Tuell convened the penalty phase with a statement: "To the counsel, for your guidance, we'll kind of follow the form that we followed in the trial. That is, there will be an opening statement from the church counsel … a chance for the church to present any witnesses. The same pattern. At the end there will be a chance for a closing statement.

"So I think maybe I should also say that in this phase, we're in a somewhat different mode in that we're not dealing with a particular narrow disciplinary provision that limits the relevancy of testimony. We're going to be quite open to whatever you decide which is to be presented in the way of evidence and arguments that you want to give to us.

"I mean it's just going to be a little more freedom … because we're talking about something that's a matter of degree at this point rather than a specific yes and no question.

"Are you ready, Mr. Williams?"

Williams: "Yes.…"

Williams rose to his feet and began. "It is not easy … to sit in the seat of judgment and hold the awesome responsibility of executing justice. You know that now. But justice is as precious a word in every language as love. Justice is the foundation of love. Justice is as important to every society and organization—and even the church, as we're seeing. Indeed, it is the church that proclaims that God is both just and justifier through Jesus Christ. That on the cross of Christ somehow, some way, mercy and justice, love and truth touched one another. In the language of scripture, they kiss.

"But, oh, the agony that brought those things together. The agony of that kiss. It cost the world the life of the most beautiful expression of humanity to ever grace this planet. It cost the world a tearing and a rending for mercy and justice to kiss.

"Beginning Sunday, we will—together as God's family—celebrate God's triumph. Christians believe that through the cross of Christ and his great passion, God was both just and justifier. The one who justifies us does it so that we, too, might become just and holy.

"Paul wrote that through the gift of God's spirit, you are now competent to judge on matters that arise in the household of faith. You will recall from Corinthians, when he was troubled that the church could not settle a significant moral dispute, he said, don't you know that you're going to judge the angels? How much more things in this life? He told them to appoint the least and lowest from among them to judge on this matter.…

"The church asks you to protect it from further harm. The church asks you to recognize that significant damage and confusion has been inflicted on this part of the body of Christ.…

"I do not believe Greg Dell wants to destroy the temple of God.… But I do believe his acts are destructive.… They hurt people who put their faith in … and have been faithful and loyal and supportive of this institution. They violate our covenant of trust, and trust is what holds us together.… They cast in doubt boldly whether our community believes what it says. They threaten the moral principle.…

"Greg is my brother, and I consider him a friend. Nothing has pained me more than the thought of hurting someone I respect, genuinely respect. I consider him not my equal, but my superior in many ways.

"But that is precisely what I will do. What I must do. And what I must ask you to consider. If the body of Christ has been harmed, if Greg is truly guilty of disobedience to our word and covenant, that is no small thing.…

"If Greg would promise me, promise you, that he would not violate our covenant again … unless our church repeals paragraph 65C, I would be the first to say, thank you. Let's go home. But he has not … will not.… And the breach grows wider and the damage more severe.…

"So I will call two witnesses: one lay, one clergy, and ask them to speak for the church.… I ask you to listen carefully, then judge for yourselves what is your solemn duty."

Sunday, August 13, 1978
waukegan · illinois

Chuck and I married several months after my appointment to York House UMC. We chose to be married on a Sunday afternoon primarily for the travel convenience of our family and friends. However, this also meant that on our wedding day the people and the work I loved most passionately all came together, making it a glorious blessing on many levels.

That morning, at first light, I rose to prepare to walk across the gravel parking lot to the church where I would lead the first service of worship at 8:00 AM. Before leaving, I laid out breakfast cereal with a bowl and utensils along with a cup, saucer and tea bag for my mother, who was still sleeping. I felt so grateful that, as facts had leaked out to her, she had reached back to me in time to be present for my ordination and now for my wedding to Chuck.

I went to the church early to deal with a perennial summer problem. As I unlocked the church doors and entered the sanctuary, I looked around and sighed. Small dark spots covered the aisle carpet runner and pew seats. It looked like a deranged farmer with a box of raisins had broken into the sanctuary and thrown handfuls of the fruit around as if he were sowing seeds on the earth.

But I wasn't looking at scattered raisins. I sighed again, wishing I could avoid this cleanup duty. I understood from past experience I would have to collect the multitude of half-dead flies that hatched out from cracks in the ancient wooden beams and walls of the building. Unable to find their way outside of the closed sanctuary in time to live, they fell everywhere, squirming and buzzing until they died. Because the church couldn't afford a full-time janitor and I couldn't trust someone else to come early enough to do this nasty job, I did it myself. Cleaning up insect carcasses proved to be just one of many "pastoral" tasks my seminary training hadn't covered.

Mom came to the 11:00 AM worship service and watched me baptize a child, receive several new members and preach a heartfelt sermon. I felt so grateful for her presence and proud to introduce her to the congregation. As I shook hands with parishioners at the end of the service, I reminded them that I hoped to see them at the wedding, which would be a few hours later.

Soon Chuck arrived with his children. Dorie and her husband lived in the area; Christie and David had traveled from Pennsylvania and New York, respectively. Stan drove from Naperville with Kathy and Mike. Friends from seminary, Wesley UMC and Frances Willard UMC (where I had preached as a seminary student) gathered in the tiny church.

I wanted to remove the paint-by-numbers picture of Jesus on the front wall of the sanctuary, but I didn't for fear of insulting parishioners I had already come to love. I also left in place the red banner proclaiming in bold letters, "If you are not busy being born, then you are busy dying."

Our family served as members of the wedding party. The procession began as Dorie's husband, Marc, his full moustache matching the color of his brown curly hair, escorted Mom down the aisle. Her scooped-neck organza dress featured long flared sleeves, and its hem swung mid-length on her shapely legs as she walked. She had decided to suffer aching feet in order to wear her white heels.

The two guest pastors followed, walking together to the front of the sanctuary. Chuck's older brother, W. Clark Ellzey (Skip), also a pastor-professor, flew in from Texas to co-officiate at the service. His wide grin and sparkling eyes looked as charming as Chuck's, and it seemed as if he had stepped out of the Old Testament with his trimmed white beard and borrowed monk's alb. My sweet-faced, dark-haired seminary friend, Kathy (Penny) Penrose, also wearing a white alb, joined Skip. Her smile reflected the warmth in so many hearts.

Chuck entered next, walking briskly and looking slim, handsome and happy in his dark blue suit. His hair was freshly cut and his full sideburns were trimmed even with the bottom of his ears (the jawline length had, thankfully, been abandoned some time before).

Then our children walked forward, two by two, one of Chuck's children paired with one of mine. Chuck's oldest, Dorie, looked lovely with a white magnolia tucked behind one ear. She was nine months pregnant with her first child, Marge and Chuck's first grandchild. She was accompanied by Stan, who looked grown up and handsome in his gray three-piece suit.

Christie and Kathy, our middle children, came next. Christie, a graceful and sweet-looking woman, wore her long brown hair parted in the middle and pulled into a bun at the back of her head.

Kathy wore an attractive silk blouse and full skirt that complemented Christie's print dress. She walked with perfect posture and looked so pretty with her dark brown shoulder-length hair and new high-heeled, open-toed shoes.

Finally our two youngest walked up the aisle. The other children had been similar in height, but the top of Michael's head reached only to the middle of David's chest. They were a charming pair nonetheless. David was slim and earnest-looking, dressed in a dark gray three-piece suit.

Michael was wearing his blue three-piece suit, his hair uncharacteristically combed back off of his forehead. They both looked playful, as if they were having the best time of all.

I walked the short aisle alone to greet my beaming groom. I had chosen a gown that seemed sophisticated and romantic: a plum-colored, floor-length, pencil-slim dress with a sheer overlay with plum and blue flowers.

The entire service felt full of the presence of love, including when our children—his three and my three—shook hands and greeted one another, "Hello, my brother; hello, my sister."

We giggled when Chuck's wedding ring fell to the wood floor and rolled noisily before Stan recovered it for me. Dorie played her guitar and sang a solo of "Song of the Wounded" by Joe Wise, a contemporary hymn I had chosen because of its beautiful words about God's healing grace. It seemed especially appropriate for all of us.

I felt great joy when, at the end of the service, I gazed into my new husband's delighted eyes and shared with him our first kiss as a married couple.

In 1983, after five happy years at York House, I received an exciting new appointment to Christ United Methodist Church in Elmhurst, Illinois, 18 miles due west of Chicago. This church was quite different than York House: suburban, largely white-collar professionals, and economically more affluent. The building was only 23 years old as opposed to York House's century-old sanctuary, and it was architecturally modern and attractive. However, the congregations were similar in that the people in both churches were full of spirit and delightful to work with.

I had nearly finished four years of serving at this new appointment when, in April 1987, my bishop (who is responsible for making all appointments in a certain geographical area) called and asked to meet with me the following day. He stressed that our meeting would be confidential. I felt puzzled.

I had seen Jesse DeWitt only from afar, as he presided with flair over the meetings of our Annual Conference. I had listened, enthralled, as he delivered stirring, exciting and visionary sermons that called the church to be more socially responsible. A slim, wiry man, he seemed to have trouble standing still for long. Now my mind raced with questions mixed with anxiety about why he would want to meet with me. And why the secrecy?

I wished that I could call Chuck to ask what he thought. He had traveled to Africa for a five-month teaching stint in Liberia, Ghana and Burundi. Calling was impractical due to the time difference, and telephone service was not always available there.

I went to my office early on the day of the meeting with Bishop DeWitt. Punctual to the minute, he arrived and shook my hand, his dark eyes dancing. After making small talk for a few minutes, he got down to business.

"Ermalou, I want to appoint you as Superintendent of the Elgin District, following Sandra Hoke when she completes her term next June. I know you need to talk with Chuck about this, so I'm going to give you 24 hours to do that and to think this over. Then I want you to get back to me. By the way, how is Chuck getting along in Africa?"

I felt so surprised at the bishop's appointment plans for me that I hesitated. I understood that he was inviting me to become part of his team (his Cabinet) of district superintendents (often called D.S.s) who would work closely with him in overseeing and supervising more than 400 local churches and their pastors. DeWitt would continue to have ultimate responsibility for those United Methodists within the entire geographical area named the "Northern Illinois Annual Conference," and I, like other D.S.s, would assist him with the whole conference while supervising one portion (district) of the conference.

Finally I found my voice. "First, let me thank you for your invitation to serve on the Cabinet. I'm grateful for your confidence in me." DeWitt nodded his head.

"Chuck sounds so happy and he feels that his work there is going well. It's hard to reach him since his schedule is uncertain, but his letters and our brief conversations have made it clear that he's being well received."

"Wonderful," DeWitt said. "He has a lot of experience and teaching skill to share." He indicated that it was time to go. "But let's have a moment of prayer first."

With that, he took my hands into his and prayed, thanking God for my ministry, for the church and for the Spirit that keeps us growing, accepting change in our lives and willing to serve wherever called. I couldn't help but notice that the last part seemed a bit like a commercial. He stood, shook my hand again, bid me farewell and left.

I sat down and tried to assimilate what had just happened. At my ordination I had agreed to itinerate; that is, to serve wherever the bishop appointed me. I felt glad, if nervous, to do this because I loved the United Methodist Church. It was an imperfect system and an imperfect institution (as all institutions are) but it had also been faithful in many important ways.

One thing that had always impressed me is that this denomination puts its money where its mouth is. I loved to tell new members about, of all things, our denominational budget. It reflected Jesus' commandment to love neighbor as self, as the denomination spends roughly half of its money maintaining and sustaining the existing church and the other half on people in need through its various worldwide missions. In fact, 61 countries throughout our world were benefiting from the more than 931 missionaries who were leading efforts to improve community resources (digging water wells, providing education, giving disease-preventing inoculations to children, etc.) as well as connecting people to God's word and grace week in and week out.

Here in the United States more than 100 colleges, universities and theological seminaries, as well as an impressive number of community centers, hospitals, health-care facilities, retirement and long-term-care facilities were all benefiting from significant funds contributed by local church members.

In addition, the Northern Illinois Conference supported its own long list of missions and social justice issues. And its pastors and grace-filled local congregations were changing people's lives with their preaching, teaching and caring. Those who received this care were, in turn, sharing God's good news with others and improving their own communities.

Personally, the church had given me many gifts throughout the years, beginning with sustaining my family financially and spiritually when I was a child. It had shaped me, challenged me and provided great opportunities and insight throughout my life. And most important, it had revealed the good news of Jesus Christ that all people everywhere are loved by God and worthy of grace.

When I became a pastor, its appointive system (which applies to bishops and clergy alike) had opened doors for me that otherwise, as a woman, would have been closed. Finally, it had shared the standard by which I believe we should measure all of our relationships, whether personal, communal, national or international: Love neighbor as self.

All this being true, even though I felt professionally and spiritually unprepared to serve on the Cabinet, I trusted the bishop's judgment and felt truly honored with his request. I also felt puzzled, though, about why he wanted me, with just nine years of ministry experience, in this position.

Soon I realized that because he focused on social justice, he wanted another clergywoman on his Cabinet. This would serve at least two purposes: affirm his vision of an inclusive leadership team and give socio-political support to Donna Atkinson, who was already serving as a D.S. with distinction.

Someone needed to continue the fine work my predecessor, Sandra Hoke, had done as the Elgin District Superintendent. Hoke had been the first woman pastor appointed to a local church in our area as well as our first woman district superintendent. As such she had broken through the "glass ceiling" for women in our conference. But she hadn't done it alone.

Her appointment had required the courageous action of the people at the Parish of the Holy Covenant UMC in Chicago. In 1975 this inner-city congregation had decided that, in order to support women in ministry, they would refuse to accept any pastoral appointment except that of a woman, an attitude that was unheard of. Paul Washburn, the bishop at the time, responded there were no qualified women available to him in the clergy pool of the conference. This answer rang true, as the few clergywomen in the conference were new in ministry and not ready to lead a sophisticated church that was a beacon of social justice in the area. The bishop's answer, however, did not satisfy Holy Covenant, who refused to back down from their demand.

No doubt Washburn resented their attempt to usurp the power the *Discipline* granted to him. But their gutsy efforts proved to be ultimately successful when Washburn finally relented, arranged to transfer Hoke from another annual conference and appointed her to be their pastor.

When the dust settled, nearly everyone appreciated her, and women found her to be a helpful role model of a powerful preacher, a formidable presence for peace and justice and an able administrator.

Along with the Parish of the Holy Covenant congregation and many other women and men, Hoke had risked a great deal and paid a high personal price for helping to secure the opportunities women were enjoying in our conference. Carrying the heavy burden of representing the worth and ability of "all clergywomen," her stress level and the expectations for her performance were high and she enjoyed little privacy. She and Donna Atkinson, both single women (Donna was the widow of the Rev. Don Atkinson), had been the only women appointed to the Cabinet of this conference before me. Only 23 had been appointed superintendents nationwide.

I would be the first in the Northern Illinois Conference who was married at the time of my appointment and a mother. I realized I could not let others down by refusing to take my turn at doing what felt uncomfortable. Bishop DeWitt had given me the opportunity to make a significant difference on behalf of all the women (and men) of the conference and beyond. I remembered I was in ministry to serve rather than be served.

However, I still wanted to include my husband in this decision. I knew it wouldn't be easy to reach him, as my calls to Africa often resulted in a recorded message: "The phones are turned off today." I tried him at 3:00 AM—8:00 AM in Africa—and finally got through, only to find that we had been allotted three minutes for our conversation and that every phrase we said would be echoed.

After initial greetings I asked the crucial question: "Could you stand being married to a D.S.?"

He chuckled warmly and replied, "Congratulations!"

An operator announced that our time was up. I so wished I could have enjoyed one of his wonderful hugs just then, but his supportive voice encouraged me to move forward.

Several weeks after my new appointment began, I flew to Lake Junaluska, North Carolina, for a national superintendents' training event. There I received an urgent phone call from the distraught Pastor–Parish Committee Chair of one of the churches in my district. She told me their beloved male pastor had been accused of making inappropriate advances to a male parishioner. I listened carefully to the facts, gave her some comfort and advice about immediate steps to take, and told her I would like to meet with her committee and the pastor the day following my return to Illinois.

After I hung up the phone, I stood in the hallway by the phone bank wall, marveling that I'd been in the position for less than a month when an issue regarding homosexuality emerged. This no longer felt coincidental. This issue had never been a focus of my ministry, but it kept reasserting itself into my personal life and my pastoral work, demanding attention.

I was already dealing with so many new tasks to accomplish, a whole district full of churches and people to get to know, and a new job to learn. DeWitt's energetic, brief appointment meeting with me plus a day of introduction to Cabinet work alerted me to the dynamics of the situation. I was being called to bring Christ's light to others but, due to time constraints, the unrealistic job description and the limits of human endurance, to do so in as laser-like a fashion as possible.

And here was the complicated, seemingly indigestible entree of homosexuality on my plate again! Meanwhile, the church, having for centuries avoided discussing sexuality in general as if it were a plague, certainly wasn't ready to seriously consider the broad ramifications of its position of condemning all loving expressions of homosexuals toward members of their own gender. In many ways, I was on my own again.

When I returned from the training retreat and talked with the pastor, he denied the charges, and I found that the PPRC tended to believe him. Let's face it—they wanted to believe him. Not to believe him would have caused unbearable chaos. Besides, they loved him, as did his wife and children.

I wanted to believe him, too, because he was one of my most gifted and charismatic pastors, presiding over a church that was growing fast, due in large part to his leadership. But given my personal history, I knew that anything was possible. I also knew I must maintain an open mind and deal prayerfully with the facts.

Soon I discovered that the accusation was formally categorized as hearsay since the offended party felt unwilling to write out and sign a formal charge, which is required by our *Discipline* to protect all parties against frivolous accusations. I wanted to get to the bottom of the matter, but since the offended party would not cooperate, I did what I could: listen, console and comfort those who were willing to deal seriously with me. In other words, I did damage control.

Although I resolved that situation peacefully (at least for the church and the pastor), I still felt uncomfortable and could only imagine what the complaining parishioner must have felt if his complaint were true.

CHAPTER NINE

Bishop Tuell thanked Williams, then asked Pickens if he wished to reserve his statement until later. He did.

Paul Lewis, a member of Wesley UMC in Aurora, Illinois, was then called to testify. He related that he had always been a Methodist, that his family moved about frequently as he grew up, but they were always able to find a Methodist church in their new location. He also said that when his younger brother died in infancy, it was the people from the church who brought food and gave comfort and support to their family. He remembered his mother going to an annual conference meeting when there was a "big issue fighting for the integration of the United Methodist Church." (He didn't reveal her stand on the issue.) He spoke of earning his Eagle Scout award with the church's help and later moving with his family to India and finding a church where people spoke Hindi. He was especially impressed with a Methodist mission, orphanage and school there.

When he finished his military service and law school, he returned to Aurora and joined his mother's church in 1978, where he still belongs. He is married and has four children: three daughters and a son, all of whom are very active in the church.

Williams: "All right. From your perspective, Paul, as a layperson, what is the impact on the church of Pastor Dell's actions?"

Lewis: "The confusion for our children, a number of parents have expressed this and I see it in my own household with two teenage daughters ... we know that when we send our kids to school we can't control the message they get. We know that when they read the paper or watch TV, we can't control the message they get. But in our home, we can control the message they get about their sexual behavior. When they go to church, we expect that our church will be faithful to that same message. And it causes enormous confusion when they open the newspaper and they see that a union ceremony that we've always told them is not acceptable is being performed. And it raises a whole host of questions not only about issues of homosexuality but also whether we're not telling the truth about other sexual matters."

Williams then questioned him about the impact Dell's action would have on other areas of the church.

Regarding the area of stewardship, Lewis testified that the two or three people who had always pledged until that year were saying, "there's plenty of places we can put our money that will give a Christian message, but we're not sure that our church is going to right now and if can't trust that, maybe we'll channel our money into other places."

Regarding church leadership, Lewis testified that his church's Administrative Board chair was resigning, "as the stories started to appear last fall, each month at Administrative Council she would bring in a new story and was very, very upset about what she saw reflected in the paper[s].... A month or two ago she announced to us that she thought she really ought to leave [her leadership position] as she starts to see positions [of Dell's support of the GLBT community] that she believed all her life [were wrong]."

He also testified that he thought Dell's actions would negatively affect new member recruitment, pastor–congregational relationships and loyalty to the appointive system. "[People are saying] if we look at the elders and they aren't going to hold one another accountable, we'll have to somehow. So why don't we just issue our own call?" Lewis also spoke of how destructive the model of public confrontation is as opposed to local church dialogue on hot topic issues such as homosexuality. He finished his testimony with these words:

"And so for me, as long as an elder remains in connection and can get appointed to a church and can serve but is not held accountable to our mutual decisions in the process, then we've lost the Methodist Church. We really have."

Bishop Tuell asked Williams to call his second witness. He replied that Rev. Awilda Nolla, who was scheduled to arrive at 3:00 PM, was not yet present. Bishop Tuell called for a short break, during which he conferred with counsel. Upon returning, he declared that there would be a recess for dinner (it was now 4:30 PM) and that the penalty phase would reconvene at 6:00 PM.

At 6:00 PM, Nolla still had not arrived, reportedly due to a wreck on the freeway. The bishop delayed the process for another full hour.

At 7:00 PM, when she still had not arrived, Tuell announced that he and counsel had conferred and agreed that the proceedings would resume with the understanding that Nolla could testify if she arrived before the end of the defense witnesses' testimony. If she arrived later, or did not come at all, she would be disqualified.

Tuell then expressed his intention, if at all possible, to conclude the penalty phase that same evening, warning those present this might be quite late. Then he called on Pickens to begin.

Pickens: "Brothers and sisters of the Trial Court, we have endeavored together these past two days. A great deal of work and challenge has been put before us as brothers and sisters who make up the Order of Elders within the bounds of the Northern Illinois Conference.

"Let me say this to you. We understand that you have spoken, particularly with regard to a legal decision. We accept the decision that you have come to. We know that you did so as a result of diligent and thoughtful consideration. Early in the process when we selected you to carry out this role, it was the feeling of our entire team that we had a very strong Trial Court. Let me say to you now, that feeling is still there.

"Although we can do nothing about the verdict, we can do something about what happens from now on. And what I ask for you to do tonight is to let the healing in our church begin. There is nothing to be gained by getting a pound of flesh from Greg Dell. There is nothing to be gained by losing an effective pastor to the ministry of our church or in some way substantially altering his ministry.

"Quite simply put, we are a church that is at a crossroad. And what I want you to understand is that this has not been an easy process for any of us. The fact is, all of us are struggling. All of us are trying to grapple with this issue and how it's going to be addressed in the life of our church. How are we going to live together as brothers or sisters? In the midst of chaos, how do we find a center of hope?

"It seems ironic to me that we are here a few days prior to Palm Sunday … that day that we celebrate Jesus' triumphant entry into Jerusalem. A day when it's easy to acknowledge the greatness of Jesus as those who had believed in him stood by him in those days. But isn't it ironic that everybody loves him then? But it's when you're down and out oftentimes that you can't find your friends anymore.

"Right now, we have an opportunity to recover and retrieve the life and the ministry of a pastor who is concerned about doing the right thing. And as you listen to the testimony that we offer, we ask that you give it strong consideration and use it to make a determination of mitigating circumstances that should affect what you decide ultimately during this penalty stage. We do so because we believe that you will make the right decision and therefore we come to you in the spirit of humility and in a spirit of hope asking that you would receive this testimony and this evidence as a statement of a pastor who is committed to doing the right thing.

"Reverend Dell has committed his ministry to not always doing what is politic but to doing what is right. And with that in mind, I ask you, let us not do what is politic for the moment but let us do what is right.

"Thank you for your work and God bless you. Amen.

"I would like to call my first witness, The Reverend Darius Thomas."

fall, 1987
elgin · illinois

Soon after I was appointed a district superintendent, serious sexual issues—homosexual and heterosexual alike—presented themselves to me. I began to wonder if my appointment as a D.S. meant, among other things, that God was calling me to help heal the important but often misunderstood and misused gift of sexuality.

One case involved a man trying to move his partner into a church parsonage. I had appointed this man as a student pastor, knowing him to be both gay and gifted. Before his appointment, I sat down with him and reviewed the troubled history of the local church under consideration. A heterosexual pastor had betrayed that congregation's trust years before in a scandal that was widely reported nationwide. Johnny Carson had even joked about it during the monologue of his popular late-night TV show. The church was still struggling to live down their negative reputation in the community. The congregation had diminished to the point they could not afford to pay a full-time pastor, which is why they needed a part-time student appointment.

After discussing this matter with the pastoral candidate, I asked if he would be willing to keep his sexual orientation private and live alone in the parsonage. I explained that, although possibly unfair to him (he had not revealed whether or not he was a "practicing" homosexual), I felt I must require this as a condition of his appointment, as the church continued to be too fragile to deal with more controversy. He assured me this would be acceptable, and I made the appointment with that understanding.

A short time later, I received a call from his Pastor–Parish Committee Chair about the "other man living with our pastor in the parsonage." Feeling betrayed, I immediately called the pastor. During our conversation, he not only validated the fact that his partner was openly living with him but also declared he felt no need to change the situation. I found his smug sense of entitlement maddening and immediately set up an all-church meeting.

When I arrived, I found strangers who identified themselves as friends of the pastor in the room with video cameras and tape recorders. They were apparently ready to use the meeting for purposes of advancing their private agenda. I informed them I was having a private meeting with the pastor and the congregation and politely but firmly demanded they leave.

We then proceeded to deal with the matter openly and came to a clear, if sad, resolution. The church was willing for him to stay if he would ask his partner to move out of the parsonage. He refused, and I removed him from the appointment.

I later had to deal with this matter on another level when he instigated a complaint to the Board of Ordained Ministry (BOM) claiming I had illegally removed him from the church. I was serving as the Cabinet representative on the BOM at that time and was known as someone who actively worked for the rights of gays and lesbians.

For instance, all who had been present had watched Chuck and me stand with many others at an ordination service in June that year, wearing black armbands in silent protest that Phyllis Jean Athey was not included. The BOM had recommended her because she was an exceptionally gifted, committed candidate regardless of the fact she was also open about being homosexual. Her approval as a lesbian was a first for the BOM, but we all knew the bishop would need to appoint her in order for her ordination to take place.

That year was not unusual in that there were more candidates recommended than churches available for appointments. This was primarily because the projected number needed, given earlier to the BOM by the Cabinet, kept changing after the Candidates' Retreat due to late retirements, deaths and other emerging pastoral and congregational needs. So the bishop couldn't appoint all who had been recommended and, determining that the conference was not yet ready to receive an openly homosexual pastor, Jesse DeWitt chose not to appoint Phyllis.

Although there were mixed reactions to his decision, those of us who stood at the service were unified about one thing: making a witness to the need for the church to learn about the issue of homosexuality and be more open to the gifts and graces of those called to ministry, whatever their sexual orientation.

Fortunately, I suffered no lasting repercussions from the complaint of the disgruntled pastor in my district, as the Executive Committee of the BOM dismissed it. Further, as I reflected on the pastor's arrogance and defiance, I became increasingly grateful I had decided to remove him. I also realized I had learned another lesson about how complicated social justice can be.

This incident illustrated as well the peculiarities of our conference. A clergy colleague comforted my worries about the complaint by observing that for some activist pastors, ideology seemed more important than people. Later, Bishop Duecker invited one of his Episcopal colleagues to meet with the Cabinet to share his personal assessment of our conference. We hoped to make use of his observations in our planning and strategizing. He seemed to agree with my pastor friend's summary and elaborated about our operating methods.

The main points were (1) No common purpose held us together. Each special interest group (and there were many) focused on its own agenda. (2) The conference ethos was one of negative expectations. A "victim mentality" was dominant, encouraging low expectations. (3) At the same time the conference was dominated by the myth that we were ahead of other annual conferences, when the reality was that we were still living in the '60s in our methods and procedures. (4) The conference also possessed a strong individualism that did not readily accept and implement community goals. (5) The conference had a history of conflict that often immobilized it.

This disappointing supervising experience and the visiting bishop's assessment became part of on-the-job learning for me as I rushed through days dealing with various church crises and attending to myriad responsibilities with little time for processing anything or resting, all the while trying desperately to move with rather than against the wind called Ruach.

Meanwhile, the sexual-driven incidents continued. One large church discovered that their married pastor was involved in an affair with his female secretary, another complained that their pastor had shown near-pornographic films to a youth group, and another church was shocked that their male pastor had engaged in multiple affairs with female parishioners. The Cabinet responded quickly and effectively to these acts, demanding that some pastors surrender their orders. Others were placed on "involuntary leave" when that seemed appropriate and if they were willing to engage in extended therapy. This helped some people, and a few recovered sufficiently to resume pastoral duties. But the bishop required that when it was time for them to be appointed to a church again, the receiving PPRC would be advised of the offending pastor's history and would have to be willing to receive the pastor.

I thanked God that most of the pastors in the district were upstanding, gifted and inspiring leaders. But I found the confusion and rebellion of a few regarding appropriate sexual boundaries difficult to deal with. Having settled my own issues before serving the parish didn't exempt me from agonizing about my colleagues' misconduct and the great harm it did to spouses, congregations and the congregants who engaged with them in extramarital affairs.

The "other woman" in most cases lost her lover (and/or her husband), pastor and church community (and sometimes her faith) when the truth emerged. These women often disappeared from the congregation and, sadly, there was little we could do to help them heal. However, we did one good thing for them and for the wives: We listened to their painful stories with respect and, when they were willing to make a formal complaint, followed up by promptly taking appropriate action with the offending pastor.

An important resource for clergy spouses was the Concern for Clergy Families Committee, created by the Commission on the Status and Role of Women (COSROW). This group provided vital information for pastors' wives who, because of divorce, were required to move from their home (the parsonage), suffer the loss of their health insurance (as part of the clergy family), and in many cases learn to support themselves and be on their own for the first time in their lives. The committee also created support groups to help them through these difficult transition periods.

Overall, these incidents emphasized the obvious: When we mistakenly and unfairly assign sexual misconduct only to homosexuals, we choose to embrace intentional blindness about the rampant heterosexual confusion and transgressions in our society at large and in the church. Further, when we fail to engage in study and discussion about human sexuality, we passively condone the status quo of ignorance, subterfuge, emotional, spiritual and financial damage as well as occasional physical violence.

One positive incident illustrated the kind of hope and helpful results that can happen when people approach such serious issues with faith and strength. It began when a courageous gay pastor, who also served on the Board of Ordained Ministry, approached me one day during our lunch break.

"Can I speak to you alone, Ermalou?" he asked. He looked deeply concerned.

"Sure, Todd. Let's find a room where we can be private."

The only room we could find turned out to be symbolic—a closet. It was full of janitorial equipment. We squeezed in, Todd shut the door and we sat down knee-to-knee on two folding chairs Todd had brought from the larger room.

"I think you know, Ermalou, that I'm gay."

"Yes, Todd, I do. I also know you are a gifted pastor and a terrific person."

"Thanks for that, but I'm wondering if Bishop Duecker knows that I'm gay? Do you think he does?"

"I have no idea. I've never discussed this with him or heard others do so. Why do you ask?"

"Well, I've just been diagnosed as HIV-positive," Todd said. "And I'm worried whether our conference insurance will cover the costs of my treatment."

"Todd, I'm so sorry about your diagnosis," I said, taking his hand as I felt tears welling up. "Thank God there's treatment these days to help."

"Yes," he said, "but it's expensive, so I can't lose my insurance. And I'm afraid that making claims for payment will cause me to lose my appointment. Do you think I might talk with the bishop about this—or is he anti-gay?" I could see the fear in his eyes.

"He's a very compassionate person, Todd. I'm sure it would be fine to talk with him. But be aware that if you tell him you're a practicing gay man, he'll be required by the *Discipline* to remove you from the pulpit."

Todd was quiet for a moment. "I can't afford to be without work, especially now," he said. "And, besides, I have a strong ministry. I love my church. Are you sure he won't take away my appointment?"

"I can't be absolutely sure, Todd, but I think he'll receive you with sympathy and with the same appreciation for you and for your ministry that I feel. I think it's definitely worth the risk."

As we stood and hugged one another, he planted a firm, wet, hot kiss on my cheek. Strangely, the heat lingered for about ten minutes. I have to admit that, at the time, we weren't sure how AIDS passed from person to person, and I couldn't help but wonder if the kiss had been dangerous. Had fever caused the heat, or was its lingering presence the sign of Spirit—just as it had been at Pentecost (Acts: 2:3, NRSV)?

Todd did risk a meeting with Bishop Duecker, who assured Todd his insurance would remain intact. No one, he said, would be removed from the pulpit unless he or she met both the requirements of being a "self-avowed and practicing homosexual." Having put those concerns to rest, Todd proposed starting an HIV network in the conference, boldly requesting that Duecker's wife, Marj, join it as an advocate.

Marj agreed to do so and offered the Episcopal residence as the network's regular meeting place. This group joined with another official committee and, with Todd as its chair, was instrumental in creating educational materials to assist those suffering from AIDS. Bishop Duecker, demonstrating his compassion, provided funding so these materials could be distributed to every local church in the conference.

CHAPTER TEN

During the months that led to the trial, I felt tension grow in my congregation at St. Andrew. Like the larger church, it was deeply divided about the issue of homosexuality. I realized many of my congregants had not had the privilege of exploring their questions and fears about this issue or of hearing new information in an open and non-judging community.

The parishioners at my second appointment, Christ UMC in Elmhurst (1983–1986), had been more fortunate, as they'd had the chance to hear a parishioner's parents speak to an adult class. Harry and Margaret, a middle-aged couple with graying hair, looked kind, earnest and intelligent when they arrived on a Sunday morning, having driven 50 miles from their home. Harry was dressed in a dark suit and Margaret in a conservative dress. Neither their appearance nor their gentle demeanor suggested they held radical views about anything.

After introducing themselves and the men who accompanied them, they shared their personal story with us. Members of the class were used to hearing local activists and political figures, such as the local mayor and other officials, address them on social justice issues. They greeted the visitors with warmth and interest.

Harry and Margaret looked confident and calm as they began. Although I don't remember their informal presentation verbatim, the crux of it went something like this:

Harry: "Margaret and I are the proud parents of four wonderful children. They're all talented and productive adults, and they live in several states, including Illinois. When they were children, we struggled with how to handle what we thought was a problem with two of them."

Margaret: "Harry is alluding to the fact that two of our children are straight and two are gay."

Harry: "That's right. And when we began to notice that two of our boys seemed 'different,' we felt terrible."

Margaret: "We felt like we'd failed them in some way. We thought that something was wrong with them, and the way we reared them had been the cause of it."

By this time, most class members were leaning forward in their chairs. Others were sitting very still, careful to not look to their right or left or reveal their reaction. I watched with some nervousness, as I didn't yet know members of my congregation well.

Harry: "At that time, along with most Americans, we thought that homosexuality was a sickness. Today we understand that's nonsense. You may know, for instance, that the American Psychiatric Association decided in 1973 that homosexuality isn't an illness at all, and in 1974 its membership voted to ratify the removal of that definition from the *Diagnostic and Statistical Manual of Mental Disorders*. But, of course, that came well after our children had grown up."

Margaret: "There had been some important studies by psychologists then, such as Evelyn Hooker's work, funded by a grant from the National Institute of Mental Health. She found there is no psychological difference between heterosexual and homosexual men. And that put a real dent in the classification of it being a mental disorder."

Harry: "But we didn't know about that study. The press didn't write much about things like that and so we, like almost everybody else, thought that something was terribly wrong with our two boys and our parenting had caused them to be the way they were. Yet we couldn't help but wonder why two of our children seemed 'OK' and two didn't. We felt really confused and hurt by the whole thing."

Margaret: "But those two were still our children, and we loved them as much as we loved our other two. So we got busy and did some studying about the subject. And gradually, we came to understand the issue better and to feel the way we do today. Now we both understand that gay and lesbian people are no different than others; they were just created as being attracted to the same gender."

Harry: "Yes, and they want the same things that most of us want: good relationships, acceptance, support and a chance to be the best and to do the best they can in life."

Margaret: "That's what we want for them too—a whole life—just like we want that for our 'straight' children. But the reality is that they just don't have the same opportunities these days, and they even face real danger if their sexual orientation is revealed publicly."

Harry and Margaret were quiet for a moment.

Harry: "Any questions so far?"

One class member raised his hand. "Did you have any warning? I mean did you have any inkling that your two sons were gay before they told you?"

Harry: "No, we can't really say that we did. We just noticed they didn't want to date girls. We didn't understand why until they told us what was going on inside of them, how they were feeling and why."

The class member seemed satisfied. No one else ventured a question, although everyone seemed to have relaxed due to the speakers' matter-of-fact confidence.

Harry continued. "So we've come to talk with you about this today, to tell you our story of moving from our attitude of uninformed non-acceptance of all gays and lesbians to an informed understanding and full appreciation of such God-given orientation. In fact, we've started a statewide chapter of PFLAG. That's an acronym for Parents and Friends of Lesbians and Gays. One of the main purposes of the organization is to educate other people about what we've learned, about the truth, because we believe, like Jesus said, that the truth will set us free."

Margaret: "We hope that others don't have to go through what our family went through until we learned better. We're here today because we want to help with that effort."

People around the room nodded in affirmation.

With that, Harry and Margaret turned to the two young gay men who had accompanied them and asked them to briefly tell their stories to the class, which they did. Then they opened the class to discussion, inviting us to ask even the most basic questions. They led us in an enlightened, helpful discussion. I felt pleased with this powerful witness to the class and felt we all went away changed for the better.

Friday, March 26, 1999
downers grove · illinois

The Rev. Darius Thomas stood and walked to the witness chair. Thomas is a black clergyman serving at First Wesley Academy UMC and married to the Rev. Penny Thomas, also a clergy member of our conference, who is white. After words of introduction, his testimony included the following statements.

"In 1967 … [when my wife and I were married in Dallas, Texas] misogyination [sic] laws prohibited the cohabitation or marriage between persons of different races in the United States, specifically blacks and whites. And that was an issue.…

"When Penny and I went to the courthouse for a license, we were not given the normal care package that other couples were given and we were sent out of a back door because, in the words of the clerk, if somebody were to see us walking out of the front door with that package, that we may be shot. So ... there was this pastor [Rev. Wilfred Bailey] ... this pastor, willfully, you know, broke the law and married us....

"Our church was a segregated institution at that time.... There's no way that the pastor could have known what consequences may follow his marrying us. Yet he valued us and performed the marriage anyway and we will be celebrating thirty-two years of marriage this year....

"Both Penny and I were ... and still are members of the body of Christ and neither of us would have ... given any thought to getting married without ... having a pastor perform the wedding....

"My faith ... had a very ... crucial role in the marriage.... First of all, we were married because we loved one another.... For me, we were challenging unjust laws anyway and so it was a part of the movement at the time. It was also ... a way of saying that I am free. I will be free, or you'll have to kill me. I've got to be free to be intimate with whomever I choose to be intimate with...."

Pickens: "After you heard that Greg Dell performed the service of holy union, did you begin to draw parallels between your marriage and that union?"

Thomas: "Yes. Those were the parallels.... In the light of my experiences and my convictions and the witness of that pastor who married us, I disagree [with paragraph 65C, the new law included in the *Discipline*]. I believe that so long as there are people who feel that God created them differently in that way that they should not be subjected to the prejudice and power of the church. Prejudice plus power directed toward human beings is oppression. And I do not think that the church, our church, should be involved in any form of oppression...."

Williams made a brief cross-examination during which he established the difference between civil and church law and suggested that church law did not prohibit marriage between black and white people.

During a redirect examination, Pickens challenged Williams' point by asking Thomas to read from sections of the 1960 *Book of Discipline*, including these words: "Recent research has emphasized the importance of common cultural and religious backgrounds as the foundations of successful marriage. It is therefore strongly urged that each young person consider carefully before becoming engaged to anyone who does not have a similar religious background. It is important that Protestant youth discuss this problem with their ministers before it is too late." [Laughter.]

Pickens: "As church legislation develops, generally we sort of get a little more insight and you'd think that we'd get better in the way that we deal with circumstances. Is that your experience?"

Thomas: "That's right; absolutely. And I'd like to respond to that at another level. There was a time when the church with biblical warrants held that persons who God created differently, like I am different, were sub-human beings. But, in time, the church became more enlightened and now the church celebrates the gifts that people who are different, like I am, bring to the church."

Then Pickens had Thomas read from the 1964 *Discipline*, which included this statement: "Whenever a minister becomes aware of a contemplated mixed marriage, he should seek opportunity to counsel with the couple regarding the potential difficulties. The couple should be helped to understand the Methodist faith and … way of life.…"

Pickens: "Thank you. Would you say that we have a cultural problem here?"

Thomas: "Absolutely … and prejudice; a culture of prejudice."

Pickens: "And such problems can permeate a church and affect the way it deals with people like you … and people who are different?"

Thomas: "Yes … and people who are different from the majority."

Pickens: "Thank you. No further questions."

Williams entered into a re-cross-examination, challenging the validity of Pickens' assertion that both of the readings Thomas had given had been from the *Discipline*. His challenged failed to be affirmed by the court.

At that point, Bishop Tuell checked to see if Nolla had arrived. She hadn't, so Pickens called Rev. Phil Blackwell, Conference Program Officer, who testified for the defense. He spoke of helping "people see that … [this] really is not a trial about homosexuality, per se, but it is a question of Ecclesiastical obedience versus pastoral conscience and that the tension is always there as a blessing from our Protestant heritage."

While Blackwell was still on the stand, Pickens entered into evidence letters of support that had been written on behalf of Dell. Then Blackwell had an opportunity to address Williams and the court directly. He pointed out the difficulty he had experienced as a new pastor in dealing with the subject of divorce and remarriage. Although the *Discipline* had changed over the years to state that divorced persons could remarry, an unwritten rule discouraged pastors from officiating at such marriages unless they could prove the intended persons were the victims of adultery. The law had been changed in 1960, but the unwritten rule was still there.

He also pointed out that the church was still going through change right now. It had changed its law, he said, after Dell had been conducting union ceremonies for 17 years. We were in this trial process, he asserted, not because Dell had changed but because the church had changed. Finally, he proposed that an Order of Elders be created in our conference so the elders could discuss issues in a reasonable way and hold one another accountable.

During Williams' cross-examination, he and Blackwell displayed some tension with one another about determining the highest authority in the church. Williams seemed to suggest it was the Judicial Council; Blackwell insisted the Judicial Council could make mistakes and the highest authority in the church is God.

Once more, Bishop Tuell checked to see if Nolla had arrived. She had not, so he declared the court would not be receiving her testimony.

Dell gave the final defense witness. His statement included these words: "You see, it is true. I would not abandon the gay, lesbian, bisexual and transgendered persons in my pastoral care or in my community. I won't abandon them any more than I would abandon children, old folks, the mentally or physically disabled, people of color or any other group that our society decides to marginalize out of fear or ignorance or for any other reason. As long as I am ordained, I will extend the full ministry to which my ordination calls me to all persons. Not in spite of their differences but in celebration and joy....

"Words have been spoken here this evening about harm and damage. There has been a lot of pain. I want you to remember that along with the pain you heard about here ... [the pain of people in local churches who oppose inclusiveness, you need to remember the] incredible harm and damage that has been done and is being done to gay, lesbian, bisexual, transgendered lay and clergy persons who are in your midst; persons whose pain is so often mysteriously unrecognized when folks talk about how disruptive and painful this issue is. Pain from a church which says to those persons, God loves you, but we're not quite sure how much we do. At least how much we do beyond platitudes and confusing statements about affirming the worth of your identity but denying your living that identity fully as responsible disciples of Jesus Christ...."

Dell suggested that instead of beginning "denominational cleansing," the Court might penalize him with a reprimand that would become part of his permanent record of ministerial service. He also suggested that we within the church live with our differences for 14 months until the next General Conference when the new law could be reviewed. He pledged that he would engage in no ministerial behavior as an act designed for public, political witness and reminded the Court that he had not done so with the Reinhardt/Eccarius union service.

"My pledge … is not to become less politically active in or out of the church. It is only to assure you that liturgical acts I do won't be designed or supported to that end. I engage in liturgy because I'm a pastor. I know your prayers have been with me because I know you. Now mine are with you."

When he finished his statement, spontaneous applause broke out, in spite of the bishop's earlier admonition. During Williams' redirect, Dell refused to promise to refrain from doing union services.

After closing statements, the Trial Court was excused to decide the penalty. They returned shortly before midnight, having decided that Dell should be suspended from his pastoral duties until making the required promise.

Bishop Tuell announced the decision, then declared the trial had been completed. People rose from their seats and spontaneously began to hold hands up and down and across the aisles of the church, crying and quietly singing, "We Shall Overcome."

Our resident bishop, Joseph Sprague, spoke at a midnight news conference in the parking lot of the church. Media microphones pressed close and lights glared in the darkness of the night, matching the darkness of the mood of those gathered. Sprague spoke to the nation and particularly to members of the United Methodist Church, the nation's second largest Protestant denomination.

"I have an idea that God isn't smiling tonight," he said, citing the time, energy and nearly $100,000 expended on Dell's grueling two-day trial. "Clearly there are no winners in a situation like this. This is the stalking-horse issue in the church today. It haunts us." When asked if he would make further charges against pastors, he said he would have a hard time justifying spending money on such trials that could otherwise be spent feeding the poor or providing ministry to needy people.

More than a hundred supporters gathered with Sprague and Dell and his family in the parking lot for a chilly prayer service. Finally the exhausted and despondent crowd slowly dispersed.

The trial had lasted two days, ending on the Friday before Palm/Passion Sunday. Neither church law nor its interpretation by the Judicial Council was found to be faulty. Greg would be punished for putting compassion above church law. My son and gay and lesbian friends would continue to be punished for living with personal integrity, their loving, committed relationships labeled as "incompatible with Christian teaching." Unsuspecting women would continue to marry closeted gay men (and vice-versa) with the likelihood that the individual partners and children would suffer the same profound damage my family had endured.

Thus, the verdict against Greg became an integrated violence against my life: theologically, spiritually and legally. Like others, I was brokenhearted. It seemed like we needed a funeral, a time to come together to grieve, to be assured of God's love and to be held accountable to use our grief to work for justice rather than to wallow in anger that would move us toward cynicism and hate.

summer, 1995
homewood · illinois

Two years after coming to St. Andrew, I had invited parishioners to submit ideas for a series of sermons about their spiritual questions and concerns. Many responded with ideas that focused on 12 issues—just right for a three-month summer series. The topics were challenging questions about prayer, evil, suffering and cryptic biblical passages in the book of Revelation, to name a few.

The most difficult topic was homosexuality. Some parishioners hoped that I would use the Bible to condemn what they called "the practice of homosexuality." Others hoped that I would affirm that we are all loved equally by God.

Although I hadn't yet addressed this issue from the pulpit of St. Andrew, I had publicly stated my belief that, along with all others, gays and lesbians are worthy and gifted children of God. Further, I believe that when we reject them as such or refuse to allow them Christian union, we diminish the Creation, the community at large and ourselves.

I decided to let this rest for a while, making this sermon the last of the series. I planned for it to lead into the class I was offering on a groundbreaking church study about homosexuality that was to be released by our Council of Bishops. Meanwhile, my oldest son, Stan, made the issue even more personal for me. He called one warm summer afternoon just as I returned from a long walk.

"Hi, Mom. How's everything?" he said.

"Everything is fine for the moment. How are you doing, Stan?"

"Fine. Mom. I'm calling 'cause I'd like you to come to dinner next Friday evening. Are you free then?"

"What a nice invitation," I said, reaching for my appointment book before committing myself. "Yes, there's nothing on the calendar for that date. I'll ask Chuck to check his schedule."

"Well, actually Mom, I'd like you to come alone. It's nothing against Chuck—I just want some time with just the two of us, if that's OK with you?"

"Oh, OK," I replied. "I'm sure Chuck will understand. What

time should I come? Can I bring anything?"

"No, I'm going to cook, and I've got it all planned. We'll eat at 8:00, so just be here about 7:00, OK?"

As I hung up the phone, I sensed something was up. I couldn't remember a time when Stan had asked to be alone with me.

The next Friday I enjoyed the 50-minute drive from Homewood to Stan's North Side apartment, especially the last stretch along Lake Shore Drive in downtown Chicago. Rush hour was nearly over so traffic was manageable. Everywhere I looked, spectacular views surrounded me. On my right, DuSable (a.k.a. Grant Park) Harbor was full of tethered white sailboats gently rocking in the cobalt blue water of Lake Michigan. Farther out, other boats dotted the water between the shoreline and the horizon. Bikers and joggers paced themselves along the meandering paths parallel to the road, getting in their exercise before sunset.

I crossed the Lake Shore Drive Bridge over the Chicago River and glanced left for a quick view of the spectacular, world-class architecture. At that moment the lights of the buildings switched on. Their mirrored reflections joined with those of variegated images of sky and clouds, all dancing magically in the undulating river water like a living Impressionistic painting.

I arrived and parked in front of Stan's building in an attractive North Side neighborhood. The evening air refreshed me as I walked from the car to the building's front door. As I climbed the stairs to his second-floor apartment, I saw Stan waiting for me on the upstairs landing. He greeted me with a quick hug, then ushered me into his spacious living room.

"Oh, I love the way the trees look from here," I said, admiring the sweeping view of leafy tree crowns through the surrounding windows. A fat brown squirrel was stretched out on a limb near one window and several sparrows hopped about pecking at bugs.

"Yeah, it's one of the nicest features of the apartment," he said.

"Would you like a glass of wine before dinner?"

We settled onto the couch and chatted a few minutes about everyday things. Then he abruptly changed the course of our conversation.

"Mom, I asked you here tonight because I need to tell you something important," he said. "I think you may have figured this out, but anyway … I want you to know that I'm gay."

I stared into his eyes for a moment. I wasn't too surprised by his declaration. Over the years I couldn't help but notice that he never dated, although he was undeniably handsome, bright and charming. A number of young parishioners had asked me if he had a girlfriend, hoping I might put in a good word for them. Yet I never pried into what I felt was his personal business.

"Stan, I must say I've wondered about this. In fact, when I was in Elmhurst, I remember inviting you to come to a morning program at the church where we discussed this issue with several gays and the parents of gay children. I thought you might use that opportunity to come out to me."

"I remember that well, Mom, and I got it. I knew you were giving me an opportunity and you'd be supportive. But I really appreciate that you didn't try to force me to have a conversation about all this then. I'm glad you've waited for me to be the one to make the decision about what to tell you and when."

"That's good to hear, son," I said, feeling pleased and relieved that I'd done something right. It had felt much easier to preach about this subject than to deal wisely and compassionately with Stan about his sexual orientation. For years I'd felt like a blind person, carefully navigating my way forward by listening intently and following my intuition, all the while wondering if my words and behavior would prove to be blunders.

"To tell you the truth, Mom, I wasn't ready to talk with you or anyone else at that time because I hadn't yet accepted all this myself."

"Really! That surprises me."

He looked down at his hands, which were tightly clasped in his lap. He slowly shook his head back and forth, then looked up again, his eyes still serious and a little sad.

"It's been difficult for me to talk about this. I knew early on as a kid that I was gay but I felt really scared about it—ashamed and disappointed, too. You know how it is when you're growing up: You want to be just like everybody else and be accepted as normal and OK. The last thing any teenager wants is to be singled out as some kind of weirdo. So even though I've quietly had relationships for years now, it's taken me a long time to accept this part of my identity."

"I guess that makes sense," I said. "The culture and the church don't make life any easier for you."

"Exactly!" he replied. "It can also be dangerous in a lot of ways. I've let a few people at work know about this, but I have to be very careful. I could be fired. Some friends have found that out the hard way. In fact, you're the first person in the family I've told."

"Oh my gosh!" I said, shocked. "I've assumed your father has been helping you with all of this."

"No—actually, Mom, I will be helping him," he said, alluding to the fact his father remained closeted.

I asked him for a hug, and we embraced for a few moments, a move that reassured me and hopefully did the same for him.

"Thank you for trusting me with this," I said. "I'm sorry you've had such a hard time with this, but I want you to know I'm very proud of you. I always have been, and I always will be. I'm especially proud you've chosen to live your life with integrity. That takes real courage. And I feel honored to be the first family member you've told."

"Thank you, Mom," he said. "Now let me tell you about my partner!" He sat back, his eyes brightening with excitement as he told me about Michael. I learned that they had been living together for several years. As he described Mike ("gorgeous," a Native American gifted in jewelry making, a great cook, a loving and caring partner), I could tell he felt as passionate about their relationship as I felt about mine with Chuck—and just as grateful.

"Well, where's Michael tonight?" I asked.

Stan laughed. "We both thought it would be best if I sprung this on you by myself. So he's visiting some friends of ours tonight. But I promise, you'll meet him soon."

CHAPTER ELEVEN

I heard the guilty verdict on the morning news. Chuck was away for the day, and I spent hours at home despairing about what to do. I had already planned my worship service for the next morning, but I struggled about how to respond to the verdict with my congregation.

In turns throughout the day, I reflected in silence, talked out loud and sobbed. Over and over again, I paced up and down the steps of the two-story parsonage and then circled through the ground-floor rooms. I stared at the barren trees in the park just beyond our backyard.

No matter what I did or said on Sunday morning, I knew I would hurt some people. I wrestled with an internal question: Should I openly express my anger and grief or hide it to care for those in the congregation who didn't share my feelings? The tension between those two options threatened to paralyze me. I wished I could step out of my role as a representative of God, yet my only claim to the pulpit was my acceptance of that role.

This would not be a one-Sunday issue; I would still be the senior pastor of this congregation for many Sundays to come. Yet I was so angry, hurt, disappointed and disillusioned with my denomination that I couldn't clearly discern—was I being called to be a long-term healer or a peacemaking short-term stabilizer? In short, I was a mess. I began to pray out loud, giving God all my pain and anger while asking for guidance.

"I'd like to tell someone off, God. I'd like to use my mouth as a weapon and shoot words into those who are injuring your Spirit within the hearts of people we both love. But I know that violence is not the way—the violence of others or my own. What do I do now, God? What shall I say to my congregation tomorrow?

"Please move me, Holy One, through my personal anguish. Help me move beyond my concern that parishioners will withdraw from this or any church. Help me get beyond my concern about how my response might impact the budget and our ability to be in mission to others. Help me move beyond any concern except to do what is faithful to you, even as Jesus was faithful."

In a few moments the Wesleyan Covenant Prayer, written by the founder of our denomination and printed in the church hymnal, came to mind, especially these words:

> Put me to doing, put me to suffering. Let me be employed by thee or laid aside for thee, exalted for thee or brought low by thee. Let me be full, let me be empty. Let me have all things, let me have nothing. I freely and heartily yield all things to thy pleasure and disposal....
>
> "A Covenant Prayer in the Wesleyan Tradition."
> *The United Methodist Hymnal*, 607, 1989.

I heard no words from God answering my prayer, but I was given clear conviction. I knew I must express my own grief—along with what I was sure was God's grief—for what had happened. And I must do it with no apologies, yet as respectfully as I could, as I had always urged parishioners to do.

The next day I arrived at the church early to make sure the Palm Sunday banners were hung and fresh palm branches were on hand to be distributed to the congregation. As I saw the palms by the entry to the sanctuary, I felt pleased just looking at them. The long and fragrant branches reminded of my Florida upbringing.

Everyone in the worship service would be invited to take a branch into the sanctuary and, when the great Palm Sunday celebratory hymns were sung, to wave them high in the air, just as people had done centuries ago in welcoming Jesus as he rode a donkey into Jerusalem. I anticipated the fun of that moment, remembering how my congregation had playfully engaged in this the year before.

As the service began with the strong chords of the organ leading our first hymn of "Hosanna, Loud Hosanna," Sunday School children in their new spring clothes paraded up and down the aisles, onto the chancel and back again, waving their branches above their heads. Their eyes were filled with excitement and awe, their singing mixed with happy giggles as 300 of their parents and friends waved back to them with their own fresh green branches. It was a delightful moment.

Long after these children were dismissed to their classes and about halfway through the service, the mood intentionally changed. This was not only Palm Sunday but also Passion Sunday, when we remember the crucifixion of Jesus. Having to create moods of both joy and horror made worship planning difficult, but I had worked hard to design a meaningful service.

To engage ourselves in the great human drama of the suffering Jesus endured, I had arranged for the congregation to participate with me in a reader's theater. From scripts provided in each bulletin, the entire congregation read the narrative part, while selected individuals read the character parts of the long story of the passion of Christ as told in Matthew: 26–27 (NRSV). The choir was primed to yell out in unison, "Crucify him!" when that phrase appeared in the reading.

It was a powerful and disturbing experience as we moved through the last days of Jesus' life, to hear again the violence he endured, and to speak aloud the hateful words said to him. Hearing the choir shout their demand for crucifixion was chilling. No one

in the room could escape the dramatic impact of the story.
And then I gave my pastoral prayer.

O God, Lent has come full force to the church today. The tragedy of death is all around us. We can only imagine, if we dare, the terror and the pain of those being bombed in Kosovo and the spiritual harm to those who drop the bombs and send the missiles. We confess that while we can and do find many justifications for waging war, even humanitarian reasons, and while much of the Bible justifies and supports war, yet we can find nothing in the life, the teachings or the behavior of Christ that supports it. In fact, we remember how he said that we are to pray for our enemies and to do good to those who harm us. It wasn't a popular word to many people, but I trust, O God, that Jesus did bring us your word. And I thank you for his light in the midst of a world of self-righteousness, judgment, exclusion and harm to neighbor.

O God, Lent has come full force to the church today. For one of our own—a friend, colleague and ordained pastor who dares to believe that you are the Creator and that your creation is good—has been told that he must cease believing you or lose his parish. This pastor, who knows that wherever there is love, you are there, and whenever you are worshipped, honored and praised in the love between two persons, he will—as a pastor you have called to ministry—affirm you and thank you for your goodness in their lives and in their relationship. Yet Greg Dell has been stopped from bringing your good news to gays and lesbians and to those of us who want your fullness of life for them.

And so, this morning, many of our hearts are broken. I confess my heart is broken, O God, for Greg, my brother in Christ, for my oldest son, Stan, for all young persons who are struggling this morning with confusion about their identity in the face of harmful judgments by our culture and now our church, and for all who feel the sting of rejection again this morning. My heart is broken for all my beloved friends, even those here among us, whose names I dare not name for fear of the judgment which will then be directed toward them.

Again, while it is said that your holy word supports this rejection, I search the words and life and behavior of Jesus and find nothing to support such judgment. Instead I hear his words that we are to love our neighbor as ourselves. It wasn't a popular word to many people and it still isn't, but I trust, O God, that Jesus did bring us your word. And I thank you for his light in the midst of a world of self-righteousness, judgment, exclusion and harm to neighbor.

I stood at the front of the sanctuary with my head bowed and continued.

I confess that, like those early Christians, we are both thrilled and confused by Jesus. We wonder how we can stop evil without becoming evil ourselves. And not understanding the answer, we make our own answer, which ignores much of Christ's teachings. Can it be, that like those early palm wavers, we too want a messiah "our way," one tailor-made who supports our prejudices, one who will do our bidding rather than we his? Can it be that when we truly see Christ, who he is and where he leads us, that we join in the demand to "Crucify him!"?

Forgive us, O God, and let your Spirit lead us, that we may lay down our nails of crucifixion and pick up our own cross and follow you, and that we may bear, with Jesus, the shame, the rejection and the Resurrection hope of doing so. Amen.

During this prayer, a dozen parishioners walked out. They included a brother of the instigator of the charges against Dell. The same man had stood during the sharing time in our service and confessed how his addiction to alcohol had nearly prevented him from continuing his practice as a medical doctor. Year after year he testified to the wonder of God's grace in accepting him and healing him of his malady. We rejoiced with him. Yet my spirit of inclusive compassion for homosexuals—whose sexual identity is no malady to be healed but simply an orientation to be accepted as evidence of God's marvelous and diverse creation—obviously offended him and those who walked out with him that morning. I had been so fervently engaged in my petition to God that I never noticed.

At the conclusion of the worship service, I was pleased but puzzled by the long line of parishioners who wished to speak to me. The line extended through the narthex and well into the sanctuary. Normally only about 10 to 15 people shook my hand and said something like, "Good sermon, Pastor." Now more than 50 people stood waiting their turn to greet me.

Many of them expressed their appreciation for the prayer and worship service. A number of them spoke of how grateful they were that their homosexual sons and daughters, nieces and nephews and friends remained in God's grace. They had struggled for years, they told me, to reconcile their love for these special people in their lives with their wish to honor what is said in scripture. They felt my words had helped them finally reach this important goal.

Many in the congregation had been aware of the walkout as it occurred. Rustling pants and stomping feet had interrupted their prayerful concentration. Opening their eyes, they witnessed angry and determined faces passing by, and they reacted in many ways.

Some were pleased at what was happening, feeling supported about their growing anger over my witness to the inclusive nature of God's love. Yet most who witnessed the walkout or who heard about it later felt incensed. I listened to their expressions of anguish in ensuing days. Speaking of one of the walkout participants, a devastated, closeted homosexual told me: "I've been friends with Jim and his wife for 25 years. We even worked together in another church before joining this one and had lots of fun doing it. I love these people. I had no idea they felt that way about me. I don't think I can ever get over this," she said, tears filling her eyes.

Another remarked, "How dare they walk out in the middle of the service! That's just plain rude, disrespectful to God and disruptive to our worship."

One person expressed what still others felt: "Ermalou, you're not going to let this limit the content of your preaching are you? I'm counting on you to stay strong. We need you to do that or this won't be our church anymore."

Still another said, "Oh, no, I've worked so hard to build up a good choir. Now all of this trouble is going to destroy all that I've worked so long and hard for. Why can't we just have peace?"

Finally one person shared the primary question that had been on my mind, too: "Why won't they just come to your office and talk with you about this? Why did they have to stomp out of worship?"

I had no answers. Perhaps the disenchanted members felt they wouldn't be listened to, perhaps they were determined to stand up for their beliefs yet unsure of their spiritual grounding or afraid of trying to express it. Perhaps they were just cowards, or perhaps they liked to be the center of attention and enjoyed making a scene. Whatever their reason, God's good news of acceptance of all was being used to create the bad news of church disruption. In the ensuing days, I invited the dissidents to talk with me; most did not. Thus, the church was plunged into the darkness of Lent both by the liturgical season and by the walkout.

I continued trying to reconcile with those open to that

possibility—and to help the congregation say goodbye to those who weren't open to healing the rift. Meanwhile, I endured the cold rain of sustained personal attacks and attempts to replace me, finding refuge in the support from many parishioners, colleagues, my supervisors and, as always, my husband, Chuck.

The warmth of collegial support also calmed me during meetings with friends who shared my shock and pain. They listened long and often to my recounting of the difficulties and challenges. And they reassured me that I was acting as a strong leader and faithful witness of God's good news.

The Pastor–Parish Committee nobly defended the gospel and my interpretation of it. Their chairperson, Susan Grove, guided the committee to deal with all complaints with fairness, compassion and competence. This was difficult work. Their efforts took hours of meetings and robbed them of time for relaxation and family gatherings.

Some of my seasoned staff agreed with my stance; some didn't but were willing to present a united front to the congregation. Our young staff members wondered what the fuss was all about, as accepting gays and lesbians was a non-issue for them. Only one member of the staff was overtly critical of my stance. His previous behavior about other issues had already disturbed the PPRC, and he was fired.

Within the congregation, the dissident group withdrew their money, refusing to pay their pledges to the church budget and redirecting their funds to special interests. They resigned from committees. Many refused to come to worship services. They began holding secret meetings. They bombarded our district superintendent, the Rev. Dr. Donald F. Guest, with complaining phone calls and inundated him with angry letters. Before long, his file on me was six inches thick.

Bishop Sprague also received angry communications and demands to replace me. However, his interpretation of the scripture matched mine, as did Guest's. Sprague referred all callers and forwarded all letters to the D.S., refusing to cooperate with the dissident parishioners' attempts of going over Guest's head. Meanwhile, he sent me handwritten notes of support and called me with encouraging words.

Nonetheless, I found it amazing how much trouble a few families could make. With the support of my judicatories and most of my staff and parishioners, I determined to weather the storm. I was thankful it came late in my ministry when I had matured spiritually and administratively. Yet those stormy years were agonizing. I had come to love those who were angry and wanted nothing more than to reconcile with them. I reached out to them individually and prayed for healing to take place between us as well as between them and other members of the congregation—all to no avail.

The dissident group made it clear I should either back off from what I considered faithful preaching or else. A prolonged power struggle ensued. After many months of this, our D.S. agreed to their demand for an all-church meeting. That proved to be a night I'll never forget.

We met in the fellowship hall. The space was jammed with people. Most were sitting on metal folding chairs arranged in rows; others were standing around the painted concrete walls that featured sayings of Jesus. The sayings, such as "I am the light of the world" (John 8:12, NRSV), had been painted there to encourage our homeless guests, who slept on floor mats in the room one night a week.

It would have been difficult to fit anyone else into the space. The sound of metal chair legs scraping against the beige tile floor mixed with nervous chatter. As I entered and sat down at the front on one of several chairs facing the group, I breathed in the distinct odor of an excited crowd. Overhead, ceiling fans whirled to distribute the summer heat.

Our Pastor–Parish Chair was poised to introduce our superintendent. She would be the liaison between him and the congregation.

A tall, attractive black man, Guest had already arrived, and his physical stature subdued those who were opposed to inclusiveness. I hoped he would assert both his street-savvy strength and well-grounded spirituality.

After being introduced, Guest offered scripture and prayer. In his strong, resonant voice, he spoke eloquently of our common church history and purpose. Some people seemed impatient with his remarks, but most received them appreciatively. When he finished his unifying statement, he invited the congregation to tell him their concerns. He pledged to listen to them carefully and to take notes in order to remember each comment.

A deluge of sarcasm, criticism and petitions quickly swept through the room.

"When are we going to get rid of this pastor and get a male pastor?"

"Our pastor accepts homosexuals. Isn't that against our *Discipline*?"

And this false claim: "Ermalou has run off all of the male associate pastors."

And so it went.

Guest listened and scribbled notes on a legal-size pad of paper. The angry, often long-winded attacks continued. I felt grateful that a number of people affirmed my ministry in powerful and moving ways. But, on the whole, most supporters sat silent, shocked at the viciousness of the dissidents and glancing nervously at me from time to time. I sat quietly, trying to show no emotional response and wondering what would happen next. I was glad I wasn't conducting this meeting. Guest continued to patiently listen and write more notes without responding.

Finally the sharing was completed. Everyone who wanted to

speak had been given the opportunity to do so. It was time for Guest to respond. I don't remember everything he said, but there are some things I cannot forget. First he launched into a direct response to the dissidents.

"I hear that some of you have been withholding your pledges to the church," he said. "I want you to know that we don't need or want your money. This church will do just fine without it.

"I hear that others of you are asking for Rev. Roller to be replaced with another pastor. I want you to know that she isn't going anywhere. I've thought about sending you the pastor that you deserve. I've thought about scraping the bottom of the barrel to get someone like that. But I'm not going to do that. Ermalou Roller is one of the finest pastors in our conference. She has been faithful and she's going to stay.

"I have heard some of you say that you are uncomfortable with a woman pastor. Somehow we never heard that kind of complaint when only men were serving the church. I never heard that a congregation didn't want another man. So let me tell you something, folks. These days the seminaries are filled with women. Their students are primarily women. Men are not seeking seminary training as much because, frankly, they are not willing to put up with this kind of stuff. So you might as well quit measuring your pastor by gender and start appreciating excellence when you see it."

The dissidents were beginning to look like deer caught in headlights as he spoke directly and passionately to them. I began to enjoy myself.

"And, by the way, your Pastor–Parish Relations Committee hired the last few women student associates because women were the only ones who applied. The male associates, the ones the Cabinet appointed, asked to leave this church for several reasons: one to return to school and one because he wanted to pastor his own church. Rev. Roller never asked either of them to leave nor did either of them express unease about working with her."

You could hear a pin drop in the room. By now smiles were spreading across the faces of supporters. Guest's words were like sunlight seeping through the gloom.

Without hesitating, he continued. "Some of you may not know this, but I was largely reared by my gay uncle and his partner. I love these guys very much. They really helped my family by looking out for me while my parents worked. So you're not going to hear me express anything but gratitude about gay and lesbian folks."

Then he flung out more words of truth, as hard as hail, letting them land where they would. "Some of you think that pastors are the only folks who can be charged with misconduct," he said. "I want you to know that, from what I've heard tonight, I believe some of you have been unfaithful members of this church. You have not kept your membership vows, which require you to support the church with your prayers, your gifts, your service and your presence. That is a chargeable offense. So you had better give that some thought if you don't want to be excommunicated.

"If any of this makes any of you uncomfortable, then I suggest you withdraw your membership here and join another church. But don't join another United Methodist Church, because we all believe in the inclusiveness of God's love and grace. So if you don't believe in that, you need to join another denomination!"

Somehow the meeting ended. I was overjoyed and deeply grateful for Guest's challenge to the dissidents as well as his support of faithful church members and of me. This encounter proved to be the beginning of the end of the storm.

It would take another several years for the congregation to clear away the emotional and spiritual debris and begin to heal. Some families did, indeed, leave. Looking back, I believe that, although this was a difficult time, it was also a glorious time. Those of us remaining at St. Andrew United Methodist Church were faithful to our calling as God's people. Even though we were severely challenged, I believe we accepted that call with grace and fortitude.

We came to a deeper understanding that God's table is a place where we are invited to share the sacrament of Holy Communion together and where all are welcome in the United Methodist Church, whether or not they are members. This symbolic meal reminds us how Jesus embraced the different and the ordinary, the sinner and the saint; how he shared God's love and forgiveness with everyone and called us to do the same.

The storm reminded us of Christ's death and resurrection while it challenged us to engage with him in our own sacrificial and sacramental living for the purpose of reflecting God's grace and love for the whole creation. And, as we attempted to do this in a very practical way—namely to meet anger with love and patience—we learned more of what he meant when he said, "If any want to become my followers, let them deny themselves and take up their cross and follow me" (Mark 8:34, NRSV).

After three years of difficulty, we were tired but unbowed—transformed, in fact, into a new community. Together we had learned anew what Jesus had demonstrated so long ago: God's grace is not cheap, but it is priceless.

CHAPTER TWELVE

after the 1999 trial
greater chicago area · illinois

The penalty imposed upon Greg Dell by the Trial Court had originally called for total suspension from his pastoral duties until he was willing to promise not to perform any more union services. Because he was unwilling to make such a promise, the penalty was, in effect, permanent. Dell subsequently appealed this decision to the North Central Jurisdictional Committee on Appeals. While sustaining the verdict finding Dell "disobedient to the order and discipline of the United Methodist Church," the Committee recognized that an undetermined time of suspension was illegal. They modified the penalty imposed by the Trial Court by setting Dell's suspension from July 5, 1999, to June 30, 2000. The Committee also stipulated the penalty could be lifted before that time if Dell became willing to relent on his stated position, or if the rule against same-sex unions or its interpretation changed. Furthermore, they said their decision neither supported nor refuted the church's policy against holy union services.

Bishop Sprague promised to appoint Dell to Broadway UMC again on July 1, 2000. Of course Dell knew that, without a denominational revision of its policy on holy union services, he and other clergy in full ministry to gays and lesbians almost certainly faced future charges, trials and penalties.

Meanwhile, an interim pastor was appointed to Broadway, and Dell was hired by Broadway UMC to serve as the Executive Director of the national organization called In All Things Charity (IATC). This was a clergy- and laity-based group whose name was based on the quote, "In necessary things, unity; in doubtful things, liberty; in all things, charity." This quote often was attributed to John Wesley, although it originated with Richard Baxter, a 17th-century English clergyman and peacemaker who sought unity among the clashing Protestant denominations.

IATC was actually a coalition of three groups working for affirmation: United Methodists for Lesbian, Gay, Bisexual and Transgendered Concerns; the Methodist Federation for Social Action; and the Reconciling Congregation Program. Following the 1996 General Conference, when the prohibition against same-sex marriages was added to our Social Principles, IATC focused on being a "counter movement to challenge this exclusive and hypocritical policy."

Many of us hoped for change. IATC urged all sympathetic United Methodists to write to the 2000 General Conference delegates urging them to change the existing policy. Thousands of clergy and laity did so and signed statements of affirmation, which were forwarded to the delegates.

My March 20, 2000 letter read as follows:

I am writing to ask that you take a few moments to hear my concerns as you prepare for the important work of serving as a delegate to the General Conference.

First of all, thank you for being willing to serve our church as a delegate. It is a demanding and challenging task. I pray that it will be fulfilling for you as well.

I write both as a concerned pastor (for 21 years) and as a concerned mother ... of three grown children ... all people whom I respect as well as love. I have served three local churches as a pastor in the Northern Illinois Conference as well as six years on its Cabinet—as the Superintendent of the Elgin District—and the last year as its dean. I have also served ten years as a member of the NIC Board of Ordained Ministry along with many other district, conference and jurisdictional committees. Presently I am the president of the South Suburban Ministerial Association—an interfaith organization that includes pastors of Homewood and surrounding suburbs.

My concern as a pastor comes from my deep love of the United Methodist Church—especially its historic understanding of personal piety combined with social justice. I continue to appreciate this deep understanding and faithfulness to Jesus' command that we love our neighbor as ourselves. While I realize that we, as United Methodists, often disagree about the particularities of what it means to love self and neighbor and what it means to be disciples of Jesus Christ, I cherish the freedom I have always felt and have encouraged others to feel to either join with or to respectfully stand apart from the majority opinion and/or the cultural consensus as we struggle as individuals and as the faith-community to know the leading of the Holy Spirit and to know God's will.

These days I fear that such freedom might be denied, particularly around the issue of homosexuality. If the recent rulings of the Judicial Council about this subject are supported, our great church will move into a place of judgment and repression, which denies the freedom of the Spirit and takes upon itself God's task of judging. Therefore, I am struggling to know how it would be possible to serve such a church with integrity as a disciple of Jesus, much less how to recommend it to others.

Further, my pastoral concern includes parishioners who are gay and lesbian and the rest of us who appreciate and respect them, their relationships and the way they regularly bless our local church through their presence, prayers, gifts and service. They also bless the larger United Methodist Church through district leadership and activities, their prayers and their generous financial support of its mission. None of us wishes to be part of a church that tells them, directly or indirectly, that they are inferior to the rest of us in any way. We know better and we want our church to declare clearly that they are fully God's children and that their relationships stand within God's grace and judgment as surely as do the relationships of the rest of us.

My concern as a mother is two-fold: what the church, which he loves and serves, will be saying to my oldest son who is gay and what it will be saying about him to his straight brother and sister and the rest of us who love him. I am very proud of Stan, who chose not to obey the cultural demands that he pretend to be someone he isn't in order to receive acceptance (as his father—my former husband—did by marrying me and fathering three children with me). Instead, Stan has chosen to live his life with integrity, doing his best to be faithful to the teachings of Jesus, committing himself to a long-term relationship with his partner and contributing his God-given talents to his local church, his community, his family and to his work at a Big Six accounting firm. In this culture it has taken courage to live with such integrity and I am very grateful for him and proud of him.

It also breaks this mother's heart that, while I officiated at his brother's and sister's weddings, he has chosen to "protect his mother" by not asking me to officiate at a ceremony asking God's blessing on his relationship. Something is terribly wrong when two people love one another, are willing to be faithful to one another and seek to be God's people that the church cannot bless their union.

Please give prayerful consideration to this matter as you

vote at the General Conference. I want to continue to be part of and proud of the United Methodist Church.

Unfortunately, our letters and statements made no difference. Every effort made by the IATC made no difference. Even large demonstrations at the conference didn't convince a majority of the delegates to vote for change. Acts of nonviolent civil disobedience, resulting in the arrest of some participants, at least made a minority witness.

The arrests were made following a rally of more than 300 people and a subsequent march around the Cleveland Convention Center, held while the 992 delegates inside were meeting to establish church policy for the next four years.

The marchers carried a banner with the message, "The Spirit of Christ cannot remain where all God's children are not welcome." Other Christian leaders joined in the rally, including Bishop Susan Morrison of Albany, New York; Arun Gandhi, grandson of Mohandas Gandhi; Yolanda King, eldest daughter of Dr. Martin Luther King Jr.; Jimmy Creech, the former UM pastor who had gone to trial before Dell; Rev. Dr. James Lawson, UM pastor and well-known activist; retired Bishop Jesse DeWitt; Dell and many others.

When the march around the building was completed, those protesters willing to be arrested stepped forward in groups of 10 to 12 to block the exit ramp out of the convention center. A sign held high proclaimed their conviction: "No exit without justice."

Police officers summoned to the scene asked the protesters to disperse. When they refused, the police arrested them and led them away. It would take 12 repetitions of this process before the officers completed their task. Sprague later said that the police were respectful and friendly. Nonetheless, those arrested spent several hours in jail, and each was fined $155.

Bishop Sprague interpreted his participation in the rally, the march and his own arrest with a statement to the press:

"I am doing this for both pastoral and prophetic reasons. It is important for those who are outside the fold of the church to know there are persons in church leadership who care very much for them."

Every significant attempt to moderate the church's stance about homosexuals was defeated at the 2000 General Conference. In every crucial vote, the majority had a greater margin than they needed and soundly defeated all positive, conciliatory and/ or compromise legislation. They rejected ordaining openly gay clergy and blessing same-gender holy unions. Instead, they voted to retain their 1972 statement that "homosexuality is incompatible with Christian teaching."

On June 30, 2000, both Dell's suspension as pastor of Broadway UMC and his service as the Executive Director of IATC ended as he resumed his role of pastor of Broadway UMC. This did not spell the end of advocacy for the full inclusion of lesbian, gay, bisexual and transgendered persons. In fact, the Reconciling Ministries Network (RMN), an independent, national grassroots organization, had been working to enable full participation of people of all sexual orientations and gender identities in the life of the UMC, both in policy and practice, since the mid-1980s and continues to do so today.

As of March 2010, 287 reconciling congregations, 35 campus ministries, 84 reconciling communities and more than 80,000 individuals belong to the network. This number regularly increases. The most recent count can be found online at the Reconciling Ministries Network's website, which publishes updates bimonthly.

On September 12, 2000, Broadway UMC adopted a "Legal Wedding and Holy Union Policy," which Dell acknowledges is not a perfect position but is "a faithful stance in a difficult circumstance." The policy states that all persons, homosexual or heterosexual, who seek union with one another, will be treated alike at Broadway. Thus, the exchange of vows that actually creates the covenant of the holy union or wedding of couples will be done outside of the church's service of worship and without Dell's participation. Later the couples may celebrate their covenant and God's grace during a worship service by remembering and sharing with the church the vows they made earlier.

At the next General Conference in 2004, more efforts were made to change the new church law. Among other things, Soulforce, a gay rights advocacy group, orchestrated a peaceful interruption of the morning conference session with several hundred people circling the floor carrying banners and singing hymns of reconciliation. Later more than 200 United Methodists stood in front of the convention center in silent witness for their desire for inclusiveness.

Meanwhile, a floating proposal was circulating inside that would dissolve the United Methodist Church into two separate denominations. Two conservative church leaders, the Rev. William Hinson and the Rev. James Heidinger, talked with delegates behind closed doors. Reportedly, those discussions included a desire by some for an "amicable" divorce over "irreconcilable differences."

Yet some conservative leaders, bishops and representatives of liberal groups rejected the idea of a split. The Rev. John Schol of Eastern Pennsylvania finally brought a unity resolution to the conference floor saying he felt he needed to block "a movement to drive a wedge in our denomination."

This resolution passed overwhelmingly, as delegates agreed that, "As United Methodists, we remain in covenant with one another, even in the midst of disagreement, and affirm our commitment to work together for the common mission of making disciples throughout the world" (published in *The Book of Resolutions of the United Methodist Church* 2004).

However, delegates remained unwilling to pass any compromise legislation. They even defeated a resolution to add a sentence to church law recognizing that Christians disagree on the issue.

When the General Conference added one million members from Africa to the rolls of the denomination, our discouragement deepened. The leader of the West African churches called the vote "a moment of great joy." Although in many ways it was, it also strengthened the conservative majority and its position regarding homosexuality.

Another incident occurred in July 2005, adding to what felt like an onslaught of conservative oppression. A Virginia clergyman, the Rev. Edward Johnson, refused membership to a gay man who had asked to join the church, even though the man had been attending regularly for some time, was an active member of the church choir and was eager to affirm the membership requirements. His stated reason for denying the man membership was that he was in an "openly gay relationship."

Responding to this action, the resident bishop, Charlene Kammerer, and Johnson's district superintendent, Anthony Layman, urged Johnson to reconsider or to allow the associate pastor to receive the man into membership. He would do neither. Subsequently, Bishop Kammerer, with the support of the conference's BOM, put Johnson on a yearlong involuntary leave of absence for what was considered an act of insubordination.

The conference action was referred to the Judicial Council. In Decision No. 1031, the counsel ruled that Kammerer's decision be reversed and terminated Johnson's involuntary leave of absence. Its reasons were stated in the digest of the case as follows:

> The Conference Relations Committee of the Conference Board of Ordained Ministry had no authority to consider a judicial

complaint. The Board's authority extends to consideration of remedial or other action on an administrative complaint. The Board of Ordained Ministry transformed an allegation determined by the Bishop to be the basis for an administrative complaint into a chargeable offense and as such did not have disciplinary authority to consider the complaint. The Clergy Session's action in approving involuntary leave of absence based on specifications supporting a chargeable offense is null and void.

So grace lost out again, this time due to a legal technicality.

At the 2008 General Conference, we saw signs of small but significant movements toward change. The conference maintained its statement that "the practice of homosexuality is incompatible with Christian teaching," but it added "loving caregivers" and "same-sex couples with children" to the definition of family. Plus, the language about church membership became somewhat more inclusive, and moderates were elected to the Judicial Council, which encourages hope for more inclusive decisions in the future. Further, the percentage of conference members voting for progressive change continued to increase.

Bishops have slowly but increasingly joined in working for change. On November 16, 1978, Bishop Melvin Wheatley stood alone in the Council of Bishops as he objected to and refused to vote for the council's statement declaring homosexuality incompatible with Christian teaching. (He made this public stand 11 days before the assassination of Harvey Milk in San Francisco.)

Two years later, Wheatley made the denomination's first appointment of an openly gay man, Rev. Julian Rush (who had been serving as youth pastor at First UMC, Boulder, when he came out) to St. Paul's UMC in Denver. During a hearing as to whether the bishop should be put on trial for heresy and disobedience, Wheatley repeated his earlier statement, saying "Homosexuality is a mysterious gift of God's grace," and "I clearly do not believe homosexuality is a sin." By 1982 the committee investigating Wheatley found "no reasonable grounds" for a trial.

In 1996, 15 bishops signed the Reconciling Ministries Network's call for change, which I and many other clergy also signed. By 2004, 30 bishops stood in solidarity with the Reconciling Ministries Network at the General Conference. In 2005, when the network met at Lake Junaluska in spite of vigorous protests, 42 bishops sent letters expressing concern and support.

As of this writing, an RNM insider estimates that 75 percent of the Council of Bishops supports change. They reflect the rapid change going on in the country. Currently five states (Connecticut, Iowa, Massachusetts, New Hampshire and Vermont) plus Washington, D.C., allow same-sex marriages. Ten other states allow same-sex unions or grant other rights. Ted Olson and David Boies, two attorneys who are long-term personal friends and sometimes political and courtroom adversaries, have joined forces to overturn California's ban on gay marriage.

This critical mass supporting change is growing in people in other states. It might even be taking place in what seems to be the last place for change to happen—the church.

Meanwhile, the UMC has lost gifted pastors and members to progressive denominations or to withdrawal from all religious organizations. Others of us continue to hold on, tired yet determined to make our voices heard, confident that this issue will eventually be resolved in favor of gays and lesbians yet mindful that emotional and spiritual damage will continue until that time. It took centuries for the church to recognize the gifts of women and black leaders. Remembering that, many of us keep working and waiting for a better day.

My son Stan speaks for others when he says, "It doesn't matter anymore, Mom. The church has become irrelevant." I'm grateful that he can step away, choosing as I did long ago but for different reasons, to live wholly rather than "holy." And, even as he rejects the church that rejects him, I'm grateful he understands his mother's penchant for working for change from within the denomination. Eventually, love will win. But on that day the victory will be bittersweet. We will all stand in the shadow of the souls who died waiting to hear God's good news of grace from the church but heard its judgments of rejection instead.

December 8, 2001
homewood · illinois

My beloved husband, Chuck, was memorialized at St. Andrew UMC on a record-breaking 68-degree day, reminding me of another time and place. The last such stretch of warm December days had come in 1975, the year Chuck and I first became acquainted.

The following year he had led the class exercise that helped me move out of my traditional homemaking role and into my calling as an ordained pastor. Now the larger church—colleagues and friends from around the conference, along with congregants and family—gathered to celebrate God's gift of his life among us, remembering that he had spent his adult years as a Christian leader and teacher, influencing not only me but also many others along the way.

Chuck had been hit by a car 13 days earlier as we arrived at a nearby synagogue for a Thanksgiving eve interfaith worship service. He never recovered.

Many friends and colleagues spoke at the service, but these were the words of Bishop Sprague:

"Chuck was representative of a vanishing breed, a generation of scholar pastors who were so anchored in hard-fought, hard-won relationship with God, that they were not blown about by every new wind that came down the pike....

"To remember Chuck is to remember one who was always

in the midst of the fray, but always one who sought to transform apparent hostility into God's gift of hospitality.… He was right about every major issue.… He, like so many in the prophetic tradition, was able to see the hand of God when many had their eyes blinded by the hands of human beings."

During the congregational sharing time, former students, friends and other colleagues laughed appreciatively about Chuck's unorthodox teaching methods and admired his willingness to continue to believe in God's future new reign.

Texas relatives described his days with them on the LZ cattle ranch. His children gave beautiful testimonies of their love with song, dance and music. Their mother, Marge, attended the service at my invitation. Gary also came.

The memorial ended as it had begun, with a jazz trumpeter and jazz pianist leading the congregation in a chorus of "When The Saints Go Marching In." This was the only memorial request Chuck had ever made. The church musical director, Jane Hindsley, quickly lined up excellent musicians for this tribute. I felt such deep gratitude that we could honor his wish.

After the service, parishioners wanted to help. A friend suggested an idea that would aid us all: invite parishioners to take turns having me over for an evening meal. Dinnertime had been one of the best times of every day, a time of reconnecting with Chuck. Now it felt like the loneliest and most painful part. My congregation responded immediately with invitations. Spending this time eating, laughing and remembering helped me through hours that otherwise would have been excruciating. Sometimes we dined at a restaurant, other times in their homes, and once at the Brookfield Zoo, where we admired the lights of community Christmas trees standing in the snow. This kindness helped sustain me for the six months before I retired.

Somehow, during those days and weeks, I sorted through our belongings, gave many things away, packed the rest, arranged for a mover, found and purchased a home and finished my ministry with people I had come to love like family. Saying goodbye again felt very difficult.

As I followed the moving van out of the church's parking lot, it seemed fitting that I had to wait for a passing funeral procession. I joined behind it on my way from Homewood to my new home in Lisle, Illinois. It reminded me of what had felt like another funeral procession long ago. Then I had also been overwhelmed with grief while driving from Naperville to Rogers Park, leaving my first marriage and daily time with my children to continue my seminary training.

At that point, Chuck and I had dared to say yes to our love, in spite of the unconventional and unexpected way love had found us. Our courage to step outside of the box of church and cultural guidelines—both suffering the consequences and reaping the rewards of a full and wondrous relationship—was fueled by our common need for companionship at the deepest levels of our lives. That, and the mysterious wind of Ruach that blows where it will.

Soon after graduation from seminary, I had married Chuck and together we had begun a new life in the parish followed by 23 tumultuous and passionate years as husband and wife. Now I needed to begin again.

This time I came to the crucible of change older and wiser, more experienced and fulfilled. My trust of God had deepened over the years, and my perfectionist approach to life had relaxed. I had known the unconditional love of a good and gifted man that I adored. My children had grown to be productive, remarkable people and had added wonderful partners and grandchildren to our family. I had served the church with all that I had to give for 25 years. I remained hopeful about life's possibilities but could hardly be described as naive any longer. Confident that I could take care of myself with a little help from my family and friends, I faced the still fresh, raw grief, trusting that in time, I would learn to live better with the hole in my heart.

In truth, it's not an easy coexistence, this mixture of grief and gratitude. In fact, new beginnings have never been easy for me, but they have always been blessed. My life experience has confirmed that Jesus' promise to us is true: God is always with us. Remembering this, I'm trusting God to continue to sustain me as I enjoy life's myriad gifts, cry a little and attend to the things I still need to accomplish. I'll also keep following the white feathers and taking practice flights until it's time for me to join with the thundering wings of those who have gone before me, as we fly freely and forever with the elusive white goose.

EPILOGUE

S even years after Greg Dell's trial, I talked with him about the event and its aftermath. We sat in his large cheerful office at Broadway UMC in the Lakeview area of Chicago on a cold Wednesday afternoon. Here, after a year-long suspension, he had resumed his ministry as pastor of the church. Dell's hair had become a bit grayer and his hairline had continued to recede, but he remained fit and energetic, his blue eyes as alert and engaging as his mind.

We began by laughing about the "trial suit" that Larry Pickens and Greg's wife, Jade, had taken him shopping for and required him to wear during the proceedings. "That was reasonable," he said, chuckling, "but I refused to wear the name tag with the label, 'The Defendant,' given to me at the trial. That seemed like overkill. I figured people knew who I was."

When I asked, he told me he had chosen Pickens as his defense lawyer because he had every confidence in his ability and competence. In retrospect, he says he feels his trust was well placed. "Larry did an admirable job."

"How are things going here at the church?" I asked.

"I feel good about the congregation's growth," he said. "When I came in 1995, the average attendance at worship was about 135; now it's 298 and still growing. My Wednesday evening Bible study has grown from about 20 people to 40 who come on a regular basis."

I felt pleased to have him confirm what I had informally heard around the conference. I knew his congregants felt loyal to him even as they struggled with a denomination that many felt had betrayed them. The church sent a letter to the conference saying that, while the time immediately following the trial was difficult, the Trial Court's decision would not destroy them.

> We are committed to continuing our ministry to all people in celebration of their diversity. We are committed to being "salt and light," first in our own neighborhoods, then to the greater community, and finally to the world. The suspension of our pastor will not change who we are or the connection we have to our community. We are also committed to facilitating change within our denomination so that Pastor Dell's ministry can continue and he can return as our pastor. We do not want other pastors like Greg Dell and congregations like ours to face the same injustice that we have—too many have suffered too much already....

"Greg," I said, "I suppose you weren't surprised when charges were brought against you. You must have been expecting this for a long time."

"Actually, I was surprised, Ermalou. I had been disappointed for years when I practically begged the media to report on the church's efforts against war, poverty and other social justice issues. But they seemed to think all of this unworthy to cover. So when the *Windy City Times* [the premier gay newspaper at the time] printed a story about the quiet ceremony I conducted for Keith and Karl, I felt totally blindsided.

"Then, after that article was printed, I received a phone call from Scott Field, who had read the piece. He asked me, 'What's going on?' I told him pretty much what I said at the trial and have said all along. But Scott was unsatisfied with my explanation and promised to file a complaint against me.

"After hanging up the phone, I wondered why he would have

been reading a gay newspaper." He chuckled and continued, "But I also thought about the sad irony of our common history. One of Scott's brothers, Bob, was my roommate for one semester at college, and our fathers attended the same high school.

"Since then, Scott and I had had an unspoken covenant to agree to disagree while maintaining mutual respect for one another. I had really valued that through the years.

"That's how it all started, Ermalou, with Scott's phone call. As I explained to Scott, the union service wasn't done as a political statement. So I never expected it to be covered by the paper, much less to have him make a complaint against me."

"A lot of people figure it was political," I said, "since you've been so *out there* about social issues for so long," I said.

"I know, but this wasn't political, it was pastoral," he said firmly. "I'm not immune to doing things for political purposes, and I'm not naive about things that have political power. I didn't conduct that service as a protest or a demonstration about issues. I had been quietly doing these services for years because it was a ministry to those to whom I pastor. In fact, Keith and Karl's union service was my thirty-third."

Focusing back on the trial, I asked how he had felt when Bishop Tuell had read the verdict.

"The verdict of guilty surprised but didn't shock me," he said. "I openly admitted that I had broken church law even though I didn't feel that I had been unfaithful to my vows of ordination. But the penalty did shock me with its harshness. After it was read, when I went out to the parking lot and all the media were there, I felt really emotional over the pain the church had created. I was especially thinking of a certain young man."

"Who do you mean?" I said.

Tears came into his eyes and I waited while he took several moments to gather himself.

"We were all disappointed, of course, with the decisions of

the 1996 General Conference. Sometime after that and before my trial began, I received an anonymous message. The writer didn't identify himself except to say he was a young man who happened to be gay and he hoped our General Conference would rescind its negative stance about homosexuality. When that didn't happen, he said he was now waiting to hear the verdict at my trial. And if that vote went against me, then he didn't see any reason to go on living, and he didn't plan to.

"I was thinking about him as I stood out there in the dark in the parking lot with supporters and the media after the verdict was announced. I wasn't thinking about my family's pain as much right then because I knew they were strong and with me and we'd get through it together. I just kept thinking about that young man…"

Greg paused again.

"I'm still haunted by that message," he said sadly. "I wish I could have responded to encourage the guy and give him some hope, but he gave me no way to do that. I think about him a lot and about all the other men and women who feel just as betrayed and devalued by our church. You know, suicide among homosexual youth is three times that of heterosexuals of the same age."

I was surprised by that statistic. "I can see why you're so sad about this particular young man," I said. "His story is awful enough, but he also represents so many others."

"Yes," Greg said. "So many…"

While Greg took a phone call, I thought about how tragic it was that the young man had so aligned his church's position on homosexuality with his self-worth that he had, in effect, given the Trial Court the power to decide whether he should live or die. His attitude demonstrated the damage the church's condemnation can inflict upon people who are already vulnerable. Called by Jesus to share God's good news of grace, our denomination had chosen to value law over love.

As we finished our conversation about the trial, Dell spoke of what was primarily on his mind these days: He and Jade's most recent granddaughter had been born in California, where their only child, Jason, and his wife, Tonya, now live.

Dell and Jade had flown out the morning after her birth and, as Dell put it, "tried to be helpful and to control our tendencies to be constantly grinning like idiots, but not trying too hard. Besides relishing our two grandchildren," he said, "these days I'm just enjoying being a pastor."

Dell asked me to tell him about my book. I hesitated, fearing rejection about the personal parts of the story. I knew, though, that I needed to risk the reaction of friends to prepare myself for the public reaction I'd receive when the book was published. I decided to tell him the whole story.

He listened attentively and at one point, almost as if speaking to himself, he said, "I never knew that, Ermalou, about Chuck and Marge trying an open marriage."

"A lot of people didn't, Greg, because I didn't talk about it with many people and never in a public way. I don't think Marge did either, but she sure talked about us, and what she said felt unfair, to say the least," I said.

"It wasn't just Marge," Greg said. "There were a lot of us involved in character assassination. Do you remember confronting me?"

I shook my head.

"What I remember was that…," then he interrupted himself. "I think there's a larger issue here. That issue is the way women become scapegoats in situations like this." He continued with his first thought: "I remember you approaching me on the conference floor and saying, 'If you have something to say about Chuck and me, you need to say it to my face or you need to stop talking about this.'"

"Oh, really?" I said. "I don't remember that."

"I was embarrassed," Greg said, "because you were right. I was part of a group of folks who were informally talking about 'this woman who was having an affair with her professor,' this kind of moralistic icon. Professor–student sexual relationships were problematic and reeked of victimization, and we thought it was inappropriate for a clergy candidate to be involved in such behavior."

"Chuck was never my professor," I reminded Greg. "He was at the Center then."

"That's irrelevant," Greg said. "The facts don't matter in these situations. We were trying to distinguish between facts and truth. That's the kind of strength you had, because you would have had every reason to just become a puddle of violated humanity. But you didn't."

"I felt set up," I said.

"You were set up," he said, "by Marge and Gary and a whole lot of folks who thought we were going to take the moral high ground. Actually, we were being judgmental, and our judgments actually said more about us than about you. I want to apologize, Ermalou, for whatever pain that caused you."

His comments surprised me. "I can understand what happened and why," I said. "I don't have bitterness about it. That is why I want to tell the story of how so many people are violated. It's not just gays and lesbians, as bad as that is; it's the children, it's their spouses, it's all down the line. I'm going to write the book honestly but with compassion."

"Yes, good," he answered. "It will be interesting to hear about this issue from the perspective of the wife of a gay man."

We hugged each other goodbye. As I left, I felt grateful that, although I had come seeking to clarify facts for my book, I had received more. Greg had responded to my personal sharing with caring, confessional words of his own, and a surprising apology—a combination that felt like a soothing, healing balm for my injured soul.

I had sought healing from God and from so many people in so many places over the years. I'd looked to comfort the broken-hearted child within me who still misses my father, and the adult woman I've become, still struggling with some of my life choices. Those efforts were somewhat but never fully successful. But now I had reached a place where my regret and sadness were balanced with acceptance and grace—and knew I could live with that.

APPENDIX

As he prepared to officiate at the Greg Dell trial, Bishop Jack M. Tuell had been well aware of the legislative and judicial events, as well as the debate that had been going on at the General Conference since 1972. He also was aware that this trial was not the first of its kind in the United Methodist Church. Jimmy Creech had narrowly escaped a verdict of guilty of disobeying the order and discipline of the church in 1998. Later the "Sacramento 68" had successfully dodged their own trial by overwhelming the system as a unified group.

Against this backdrop, the church-at-large was aware of Bishop Tuell's open bias against the practice of homosexuality—a bias the Dell trial would both challenge and change.

The story of his dramatic change of heart swept through the church when, following the trial, Tuell preached a sermon at his home church entitled "God Is Doing a New Thing: The United Methodist Church and Homosexuality."

On April 7, 2000, the *United Methodist Reporter* (an independent weekly newspaper for United Methodists and other people of faith) printed his sermon. The article began with the editor's note stating that Bishop Tuell had served as guest preacher on February 20 at the Des Moines, Washington, United Methodist Church. Tuell told the *Reporter* he had had no idea what he might preach about that Sunday, but when he read the Common Lectionary for that day (Isaiah 43:18–25, NSRV), Verse 19 "just jumped off the page" at him, and he felt he had to preach

193

this sermon. The sermon was submitted to the *United Methodist Reporter* by Des Moines UMC members, edited for publication with the bishop's permission, and printed as follows:

Religion has never been known as a force at the cutting edge of doing new things. "Avant garde" has not been a phrase used to describe the church throughout history. Rather, the church is usually perceived as a conserving force, seeking to retain the traditional values that have come from the past.

This is shown in the respect and honor we give the Holy Bible, a document written several millennia ago. It is seen in the ancient customs of Orthodox Christians, from time-honored liturgies to the unchanging clerical vestments of its clergy. Christians recite ancient creeds weekly in churches around the world.

All of this is good. There is truth and value at the center of religious faith which is unchanging and ought to be honored and revered. John Wesley recognized this in placing tradition as one of the four guidelines for us, along with scripture, experience and reason.

God is ever ready

But, our text, Isaiah 43:19, reminds us that God is ever ready to do a new thing. The God we Christians worship is not a static God, capable only of speaking to us from 2,000, 3,000 or 4,000 years ago. Rather, God is living, alive in this moment, revealing new truth to us here and now, in this year of our Lord 2000.

God is revealing new truth in many areas of life. One that is increasingly clear is that God is speaking to us through the issue of homosexuality.

I am aware that many people are uncomfortable even mentioning this matter and wish it would just go away. I am aware of that because I have felt exactly the same way.

I am also aware that it is not the most important issue the United Methodist Church faces. The most important issue is to make disciples, to share the love of God in a world that is hurting. But homosexuality is the most volatile and potentially divisive issue we face, and I believe that God is about to do a new thing among us.

The new thing that God is doing in our midst right now is to show us that homosexuality is not simply an act or acts of willful disobedience to God's law and commandments, but it is a state of being. It is an identity that God has given to some of God's children. It is who they are.

How does this assertion—this new thing—stand up against John Wesley's four tests of Christian truth: scripture, tradition, experience and reason?

Scripture: Condemnations of homosexual activity appear twice in the Book of Leviticus and once in the Book of Romans. One in Leviticus indicates that death is the penalty for such acts. In truth, there are instances of homosexual acts that should be condemned. I do not doubt that the writer of Leviticus and the Apostle Paul had good reason to write as they did.

But when we turn to scripture, we need to turn to the whole of scripture. When we do that, the central and overwhelming message is God's inclusive love for all of humankind.

"Gospel in a nutshell"

Scholars of all opinions have agreed that one verse of scripture is truly the "Gospel in a nutshell"—the beloved John 3:16: "God so loved the world that he gave his only Son that everyone who believes in him may not perish but have eternal life." (NRSV) The sovereign message of the Bible is

God's redeeming, all-powerful love that overrides all else, and places specific prohibitions into the context of the time, place and situation for which they were written.

Tradition: Regarding homosexuality, it is not so much that tradition has been actively against it, but that tradition has been actively covering it up. The tradition is that it is a taboo subject—shrouded in mystery—unspeakable—unmentionable—a subject to be crammed down into the nether regions of our consciousness and forgotten. As a consequence, our real tradition is ignorance. So to that extent, church tradition doesn't help much.

In another way, however, we Christians have a long tradition of change.

Some 150 years ago, in many of our churches, Methodists believed slavery was scriptural and ordained by God.

Until 1920, the Methodist Church in its *Discipline* prohibited (or tried to prohibit) "dancing, theater-going and card-playing."

The church has had a long, long tradition of finally sorting out what is truly important over what is either incorrect or only marginally important. In the long run, we have always been able to discern when God is doing a new thing in our midst. This capacity to change is among the noblest of our traditions.

Experience: Of all the four tests of Christian truth, experience is in some ways the deepest and most far-reaching. It is the force that can move us when nothing else can.

John Wesley was an academic, legalistic, guilt-ridden and slightly repulsive Anglican priest before he experienced the love of God in his heart of hearts—before his heart, as he wrote, was "strangely warmed." The experience turned his life around. It made the difference between his ending up a forgotten cleric of the Church of England and becoming what he is—a man remembered, respected and followed by millions, one of the great spiritual fathers of the human race.

What is the role of experience in the issue we speak of today?

It is the personal encounter with the anguish, the pain, the hurt, the suffering and the despair which harsh and judgmental attitudes can have on people of homosexual orientation.

How does this encounter come about? One way is when parents realize that their child is a person of homosexual orientation. They share intensely and intimately in the struggle, perhaps the denial, often the anguish, but ultimately the acceptance of the child whom they bore and whom they love. It is little wonder that such parents gather together with others in groups such as PFLAG (Parents, Families and Friends of Lesbians and Gays) to bring about understanding and change. They have experienced firsthand some of the deep, deep hurt that accompanies this issue in our church and in our society.

Prevailing view

In my own case, based on my limited understanding, I went along with the prevailing view, although never including any hatred. I said to myself, "After all, God created men and women different, complementary to one another physically and perhaps emotionally. From my viewpoint as a heterosexual person, heterosexuality must be what God expects of all His creation." It was just common sense to me.

I was wrong. Experience showed me that I was wrong.

Actually, several experiences were at work. A year ago, when Bishop Joseph Sprague (Chicago area) asked me to come and preside over a church trial, experience made its compelling points with me.

The Rev. Gregory Dell was pastor of the Broadway United Methodist Church in Chicago, a congregation made up of about 40 percent gay and lesbian members situated in a community of similar make-up. Under the law of our denomination, Rev. Dell was charged with "disobedience to the order and discipline of the United Methodist Church" for conducting a service of holy union for two members of his congregation, two gay men.

These two men were active in their church as ushers, finance committee members and regular participants. They had been living as partners for several years, but had been having trouble in their relationship. They came seeking spiritual counsel from their pastor, and they wanted to have some kind of service of prayer or blessing of their commitment. They felt it would strengthen them and make them better partners. Rev. Dell agreed to conduct a small, informal service, which took place in September 1998.

The facts of the case were never contested. For conducting this service, the trial court found him guilty and suspended him from the exercise of ministry. Ecclesiastically speaking, the decision was correct.

As I understand the Spirit of God, it was wrong.

Trial of caring and able minister

For two long days I watched this trial of a dedicated, energetic, compassionate, caring and able minister with 30 years of loyal service to our church. This experience, along with other experiences I am sure, caused me to change my mind.

I began to see the new thing God is doing.

Reason: Reason cuts both ways. For a long time, reason

had told me that God's creation of male and female ruled out anything but heterosexuality. But reason enriched by experience began to tell me otherwise.

I had often taken issue with arguments that equated prejudice against homosexuality with prejudice against race. I took issue because race was clearly a condition one was born with, while homosexuality involved behavior which is subject to human will. Having said that, was it reasonable to believe that God would create some humans with an orientation toward the same gender, put within them the same strong drive of sexuality which is present in heterosexual persons, and then decree that such a drive must be absolutely repressed and denied?

This not only defies reason, but is cruel, unfeeling and arbitrary—qualities foreign to God as we know God in Jesus Christ.

Therefore, reason supports a belief that God is in the process of doing a new thing.

At the trial of Gregory Dell, the two men who were the participants in the service of union appeared as witnesses. On the stand, in response to questions, one man told about his father, a pastor in the Missouri Synod Lutheran Church, one of the most conservative denominations in America. He had asked his father to conduct the holy union service. The father had regretfully declined, on the basis of his denomination's position, yet he attended the service. Afterward, at the reception, the father led in a public prayer of blessing for his son and his partner.

Whatever our beliefs about homosexuality, can we as Christians do any less than to affirm the committed relationships of our sisters and brothers in Christ?

In a few weeks, 992 delegates will gather in Cleveland for the General Conference, marking 216 years of our church's life. These are good people, dedicated United Methodist Christians who are earnestly seeking God's will for our church. They have been elected by their fellow clergy and laity from all over the world and entrusted with a heavy responsibility. They will have different perspectives on this and many issues facing them.

It is impossible to predict what actions they may take, because the Spirit moves at its own pace—"the wind bloweth where it listeth" (John 3:8).

But I believe that if the delegates are listening carefully, above the competing pressures of this group that they will hear the still, small voice whisper, "I am doing a new thing," and they will respond faithfully.

BIBLIOGRAPHY

Affirmations of a Dissenter. Sprague, C. Joseph. Nashville, Tennessee: Abingdon Press, 2002.

The Book of Discipline of the United Methodist Church. Nashville, Tennessee: The United Methodist Publishing House, 1972.

Christ and the End of Meaning: The Theology of Passion. Hessert, Paul. Rockport, Massachusetts: Element, 1993.

"Human Rights and the Golden Rule." Mollenkott, Virginia Ramey. *Christianity and Crisis* 47, November 9, 1987, 383–385.

Eerdmans' Handbook to the History of Christianity. Dowley, Dr. Tim, ed. Berkhamsted, Herts, England: Lion Publishing, 1977.

The Book of Resolutions of the United Methodist Church. 2004, English Edition, Abingdon Press, 1/2005.

The God Who Fell From Heaven. Shea, John. Allen, Texas: Argus Communications, 1979.
"A Prayer to the God Who Fell From Heaven" is reprinted in this book with permission.

The Holy Bible, New Revised Standard Version. Nashville, Tennessee: Graded Press, Thomas Nelson Publishers for Cokesbury, 1990.

The Jerusalem Bible. Garden City, New York: Doubleday & Company, Inc., 1966.

The Oxford Illustrated History of Christianity. McManners, John, ed. New York: Oxford University Press, 1990.

Servitude and Freedom. Dean, Jonathan. London: Epworth Press, 1989.

The United Methodist Church Re: The Matter of the Reverend Gregory R. Dell, Vol. I, II and III, from the records of The Northern Illinois Conference of The United Methodist Church, March 26–March 27, 1999.

"Covenant Prayer in the Wesleyan Tradition." Nashville, Tennessee: The United Methodist Publishing House, *The United Methodist Hymnal Book of United Methodist Worship,* 607, 1989.

The United Methodist Reporter, April 7, 2000—November 4, 2009.

The White Goose. Tudor, Tasha. New York: Oxford University Press, 1943.